PRAISE FOR *WORRY*

"My favorite author has written this excellen⸏ ⸏⸏⸏ who struggle
with fear, worry, and anxiety. Trust me, I have ⸏ ⸏⸏ all the Bible verses on these
subjects, but what I need today is a friend and coach to walk me to victory over
these paralyzing sins. I encourage you to grab a copy of *Worry Less, Live More*—
and while you are at it, get another copy for a fellow worrier!"

    —Greg Vaughn
       Emmy Award–winning film producer; author, *Letters
       from Dad*; and founder, Grace Ministries

"We are in quite a predicament. Jesus tells us that He is life. The living water.
The way to eternal life. Yet, feeling alone in our frailty, we sometimes experience very little of the life He speaks of, overwhelmed by the seas of worry,
doubt, and fear. In *Worry Less, Live More*, Robert J. Morgan—through powerful
Scripture and challenging life experiences—gives us real, spiritual insights that
we can cling to. Allow these words to take you by the hand and lift you out of
the seas of worry to the life you long to live."

    —Matt Markins
       President, Awana Global Ministries

"Unexpected life changes. Sleepless nights. Fear of the unknown. Real life that
many of us face more often than we'd like. As I read Robert Morgan's *Worry
Less, Live More*, with his compassionate unpacking of the timeless words of the
apostle Paul, God's eternal truths once again brought calm and comfort and
well-being to my soul. Journeying from *rejoicing* to *requesting* to *recollecting*
to *resting*, Robert tenderly guides the reader to the destination that Paul, no
doubt, had intended: a peace-filled confidence in the trustworthiness of our
loving God."

    —Ann Mainse
       Heart to Heart Marriage & Family Ministries and former
       TV host, *100 Huntley Street* and *Full Circle*

"Worry is a common experience of human existence. In his book *Worry Less,
Live More*, Robert Morgan wisely applies the antiworry medicinal ointment of
God's Word, found in Philippians 4:4–9. Morgan masterfully examines this key
passage, principle by principle, to help the reader have less anxiety and more
peace. *Worry Less, Live More* was a big help to me. Definitely a must-read!"

    —Moises Esteves
       Vice president, International Ministries Child Evangelism Fellowship˙

"In *Worry Less, Live More*, Robert Morgan brings his calm authority to speak gently to the lives of anxious and fretting people—helping us place our scared hands into the security of our Savior's scarred hands."
—Peter W. Rosenberger
Author, radio host, and thirty-year caregiver

"One of today's most prevalent problems in our 'high tech' society is stress. We are all beset by anxiety and worry at times, and, if we are honest, we so often allow it to dominate our attitudes, thought processes, and behavior. It can ruin relationships, businesses, and families, and can eat away at our quality of life.

"Pastor Rob Morgan has now produced one of the most valuable and insightful books I have ever read tackling this very real and present problem. Based on Philippians 4:4–9, it is intensely practical, personal, and relevant."
—Dr. W. E. G. (Bill) Thomas
Former president of the Gideons International and Consultant Surgeon

"*Worry Less, Live More* is an incredibly timely message for the culture in which we live. As so many people are gripped by fear and anxiety, this book offers hope that is found in the steadfast truth of God's Word. Rob's personal stories and courageous transparency let us know that this is not merely an exercise in study. Rather these are insights and revelation born out of his own personal and, at times, painful journey. I believe this is a book you will want to keep close for years to come. It's not just a great read, it's a guide to finding hope and freedom every day."
—Daniel Floyd
Senior pastor, Lifepoint Church; president, Lifepoint
College; and author, *Living the Dream*

"If you've been worried about locating a helpful biblically based book dealing with worry and anxiety, your worries are over! Seriously. Here it is in Robert Morgan's important work on the subject. Wisdom, insight, and balance exude from these pages. Anyone and everyone, no matter your situation, will be blessed, helped, and encouraged by reading it."
—Phil Roberts
International Director of Theological Education, Global Ministries Foundation

"Dr. Robert and I are friends . . . and some of our best conversations are through the reading of his books . . . and this one makes me want to *live more* . . . and worry less!"
—Dennis Swanberg
America's Minister of Encouragement

"Rob Morgan is a master at taking complex biblical subjects and truths and beautifully dissecting them in terms that are applicable and life-changing for the believer. So many people today are crippled by fear, worry, and anxiety, and the need for the practices outlined in *Worry Less, Live More* has never been greater. This is a powerful blueprint and dynamic guide to a life filled with peace and purpose."
—John Bolin
    Minister of Worship & Arts, Houston's First Baptist Church

"Robert J. Morgan, in *Worry Less, Live More,* has provided a wonderfully readable prescription from the Scriptures, especially from Philippians 4:4–9, to help us overcome the debilitating, paralyzing, stomach-churning, faith-quenching effects of worry. It is safe to say that we all could live better lives with less worry.

"This volume points us to a better life, not through a quick-fix but by a commitment to biblical practices that will counter our habits of worry and replace them with habits that lead to the peace of God and an awareness of the presence of the God of peace. The book is filled with helpful textual comments, personal insights, and apt illustrations. The study guide also enables us to go deeper and further in applying the insights presented, translating them into practice. This book is a great read and, by God's grace, a transforming read for those who not only worry regularly but also worry rarely, and that includes most of us!"
—David Olford
    President, Olford Ministries International, Inc.

WORRY LESS, LIVE MORE

OTHER BOOKS BY ROBERT J. MORGAN

WORRY
LESS,
LIVE
MORE

God's Prescription for a Better Life

ROBERT J. MORGAN

W Publishing Group

An Imprint of Thomas Nelson

Published in Nashville, Tennessee, by W Publishing, an imprint of Thomas Nelson.

Published in association with Yates & Yates, www.yates2.com

Thomas Nelson titles may be purchased in bulk for educational, business, fund-raising, or sales promotional use. For information, please e-mail SpecialMarkets@ThomasNelson.com.

ISBN 978-0-7180-7430-2 (eBook)
ISBN 978-07852-1661-2 (IE)

Library of Congress Control Number: 2017946592

ISBN 978-0-7180-7961-1

Printed in the United States of America

17 18 19 20 21 LSC 10 9 8 7 6 5 4 3 2 1

To my sister Ann

Do not be anxious about anything, but in every situation, by prayer and petition, with thanksgiving, present your requests to God.

—PHILIPPIANS 4:6

CONTENTS

CONTENTS

HOW TO BURY WORRY
BEFORE WORRY BURIES YOU

Amazon keeps track of your highlights. When e-book owners mark sentences, the online retailer knows and notes it. Recently Amazon released a list of the most popular passages in some of its bestselling books, such as *The Hunger Games*, the Harry Potter series, and *Pride and Prejudice*. Also released, the most highlighted passage in the Holy Bible.[1] I expected America's favorite biblical portion to be John 3:16, Psalm 23, or the Lord's Prayer in Matthew 6:9–13. But, no, it was a less prominent text, but one that's striking a deep cord in today's worried world. It was Philippians 4:6–7:

> Do not be anxious about anything, but in every situation, by prayer and petition, with thanksgiving, present your requests to God. And the peace of God, which transcends all understanding, will guard your hearts and your minds in Christ Jesus.

This is a passage I've underscored in my own Bible, and it's a portion of a paragraph I've memorized from the book of Philippians. These words shore up my sanity, because I've battled anxiety from childhood. I have a journal full of war stories to prove it. Nothing grips my spirit like worry. It's like a spider spinning webs of worry in my mind and tightening the strings, and if it pulls hard enough it almost draws me, at its worst moments, into fetal levels of fear.

I'm sorry to confess such a thing, because I'm a long-tenured Christian who's memorized virtually every verse in the Bible about worry and about peace. But I inherited a stray genetic particle from my mother's side of the family, and that gene sometimes mutates into a germ that wreaks havoc with my nervous system. I remember my mom standing on the porch of our home in Elizabethton, Tennessee, wringing her hands when ambulances raced up highway 19-E in the direction of our apple orchard, twenty miles away. Thousands of people lived up that road, but my mother always worried my dad had suffered an accident.

As a child, I anguished over misplaced library books, and my first panic attacks came when I had to give oral reports in school. A set of paralyzed lungs doesn't bode well for someone wanting to become a public speaker. If I had time, I'd tell you about the moment in high school when I barreled through an acute panic attack while onstage and, by God's grace, emerged through the experience with nearly all fear of public speaking gone. But that's another story. Suffice to say, few of my other anxieties have vanished so abruptly. It's tough to get through the social pressures of school, the insecurity of dating and courtship, and the changes required for marriage when you're too insecure to talk to people or risk rejection. One tends to burrow into one's own world. I like it in my own world—I'm an introvert—but not if I'm padlocked in there by worry.

I can't blame it all on DNA. Worry, which is essentially a strain of fear, is a rational response to real pressures and problems. Life is harder than we expect, and even the Lord Jesus, the Prince of Peace Himself, admitted "each day has enough trouble of its own" (Matthew 6:34). He said, "In this world you will have trouble" (John 16:33). On one occasion, He even said, "Now my soul is troubled, and what shall I say?" (John 12:27).

Our souls are easily troubled. The world and its trials seem to be getting worse. In nearly forty years of pastoral counseling, I've seen a lot of changes in our culture, and it seems to me we're at a flood stage of angst. People are anxious, and everyone seems increasingly tense and taunt. We're overextended, running on empty, and often running late. We're worried and we're weary. One moment we're alarmed about global politics and the next we're frustrated with a clogged commode or a cranky boss. Stress keeps us on pins and needles from dawn to darkness.

Anxiety disorders comprise the most common mental illness in America. Officially they affect 18 percent of the adult population, but 100 percent of us worry about life every day. We fret and fear as we face anxious moments, and there's a strain over everything we do, even when we're having fun. I'm writing these words on a balcony in Naples, Florida, overlooking the Gulf of Mexico. Below me are palm trees, sea gulls, a lovely pool, and a placid ocean with soft rhythmic waves. Yet worry never takes a vacation. There's seldom a time when I feel totally free from inklings of fear, and even now I have a nagging feeling of foreboding about things back home.

We need professional counselors, therapists, doctors, and people with giftings of wisdom to help us. Mental illness is treatable at all its levels, and modern science offers helpful solutions. Nutrition, exercise, rest, and good habits make big differences in how we handle stress. Prescribed medication, used wisely, can play a role in our healing. The right therapists and counselors can be literal lifesavers.

But medical treatment alone is incapable of reaching the hidden depths of the soul. We need a house call from the Great Physician and a good dose of His therapeutic truth. The Bible is our Lord's prescription pad, and meditation helps more than medication. The frequent contemplation of Scripture heals the mind better than the wisest counselor or the newest drug. To steady our minds in the storm, medical and psychological treatment programs must be anchored on a rock that keeps the soul steadfast and sure.

As Philippians 4:4–9 tells us, the missing pieces for most people are the peace of God and the God of peace. On the following pages, I want to lead you through these verses, for they constitute the Bible's premier passage on the subject of anxiety. This is God's most definitive word about overcoming anxiety and experiencing His overwhelming peace, and that's why it's currently America's go-to passage of Scripture.

It's been of great help to me.

It's time for you to wage war on worry with the weapons provided in God's unfailing Word. On the basis of Scripture, you can live more, worry less, and give each day a happier turn.

You can bury worry before worry buries you.

"IN EVERY SITUATION"

Let me tell you of a man with whom I'm familiar. He was an energetic worker who left home to roam the globe as a spiritual ambassador, a missionary. Traveling to a picturesque corner of the Mediterranean, he came to a port on the Aegean, beautiful in its setting, famous for its grapes, wine production, and white cheese. Sailors, importers, exporters, students, and philosophers from across Europe and Asia flowed through the gates and harbors of this city, and its population was a melting pot of humanity. Fishermen and financiers were equally at home within its borders. Yet it was a dark place, a city with no spiritual light. It was a city badly needing hope, needing a church.

My friend, an experienced missionary strategist, was as dedicated as anyone you've seen. As he explored the neighborhoods of the city, his heart yearned within him, and he instinctively saw the possibilities of launching a meaningful ministry. The city was a virtual open door for humanitarian aid and evangelism. People were searching for some good news, and the missionary could have done a great work there.

But, alas, it came to naught. Something stopped this man in his tracks, and he abandoned the work before it even started. He left the city abruptly, the work undone, the door unopened. The problem wasn't related to politics or persecution or finances or failing health. There were no issues with his passport or visa, no official objections to his work, no legal challenges, and no bullying.

The man simply suffered an anxiety attack triggered by an event far away, and at the moment of greatest opportunity, his emotions were hijacked by a wave of worry that robbed him of his ability to concentrate. He became so obsessed by his distress that he could not function. In a state of jittery panic, the man packed his bags and moved on like a vagabond, unable to focus, unable to pursue his work, unable to find peace, hoping to hear good news further down the line.

He later described what happened to him like this:

> Now when I went to Troas to preach the gospel of Christ and found that the Lord had opened a door for me, I still had no peace of mind, because I did not find my brother Titus there. So I said goodbye to them and went on to Macedonia. . . . When we came into Macedonia, we had no rest, but we were harassed at every turn—conflicts on the outside, fears within. (2 Corinthians 2:12–13 and 7:5)

The missionary who suspended his work in Troas was the apostle Paul. He grew so worried about the problems in his signature work in distant Corinth that he couldn't zero in on the possibilities in Troas. Paul had expected Titus to meet him in Troas with updates and, he hoped, with better news. But Titus never showed up, and Paul couldn't concentrate on the work at hand because of fears within and uncertainties afar.

To me, this is a remarkable admission. It shows the human side of a great biblical hero. It indicates the apostle was high-strung, full of nervous energy, and predisposed toward anxiety. He battled "fears within" as acutely as he battled "conflicts on the outside."

He's not alone. When a successful actress was recently interviewed by *Glamour* magazine, the reporter asked her why she was reclusive, why she didn't go out and have more fun, why she seldom partied. The young celebrity replied, "It's sad, actually, because my anxiety keeps me from enjoying things as much as I should at this age."

"Really?" said the journalist. "I know a lot of young women suffer from anxiety. It's brave of you to talk about it."

The starlet explained, "[I take] pills, long-term pills . . . It makes me tired all the time. Anxiety, it just stops your life."[1]

Perhaps you know from personal experience how anxiety in its many forms can stop or retard your joy, stamina, enthusiasm, confidence, and wellness in life. Someone defined worry as a small trickle of fear that meanders through the mind and cuts a channel into which all other thoughts are drained.[2]

Anxiety is a mode of worry, a load of care, a sense of unease, and a nervous strain that coats our personalities like enamel. It's disquiet and dis-ease in our souls. Sometimes it's nothing more than a flutter or a knot in our stomachs; other times it manifests itself in panic attacks or posttraumatic stress episodes; often we're gripped by fistfuls of fear that overwhelm our circuits.

According to the *New York Times*, Americans are among the most anxious people on earth. The *Times* reported a study by the World Mental Health Survey that found Americans to be the most anxious people in the fourteen nations covered by the research. Americans were significantly more anxious than residents of nations like Nigeria, Lebanon, and Ukraine. We spend billions of dollars every year on antianxiety medications and additional millions to fund research into the causes and cures for anxiety disorders.[3]

One recent study suggested that children who are picky eaters might later be more prone toward anxiety.[4] Another study suggests that stress during childhood can affect the makeup of bacteria in our stomachs and intestines and could influence our mental health and trigger anxiety.[5]

Other experts study the relationship between anxiety and genetics. Researchers at the University of Wisconsin–Madison reported that a study of monkeys revealed some of them had a more "anxious temperament" than others, and the scientists were able to find some hereditary linkage. According to a report in the *Proceedings of the National Academy of Sciences*, about 30 percent of a human's anxiety can be attributed to inherited factors. That means, the researchers note, that 70 percent of our anxieties can be affected by changing our outlooks and habits.[6]

Time magazine recently devoted its cover story to teenage anxiety, and the headline was: "The Kids Are Not All Right: American teens are anxious, depressed, and overwhelmed." The article pointed out that today's adolescents "are the post-9/11 generation, raised in an era of economic and national insecurity. They've never known a time when terrorism and school shootings weren't the norm. They grew up watching their parents weather a severe recession, and, perhaps most importantly, they hit puberty at a time when technology and social media were transforming society."

One expert said, "If you wanted to create an environment to churn out angsty people, we've done it."

One teenager explained, "We're the first generation that cannot escape our problems at all. We're all like little volcanoes. We're getting this constant pressure, from our phones, from our relationships, from the way things are today."[7]

The magazine failed to ascribe any blame to secularism with its despair-inducing implications. We've had several generations of children flowing through the pipeline of a secular educational system where God and Scripture and prayer are treated as banned substances, where the spiritual life of students is nonexistent, and where young people are indoctrinated with the hypothesis they are nothing but mutated molecules of primordial sludge that somehow evolved into carbon beings with no ultimate purpose, destined to quickly perish without hope in a universe that doesn't care. Educators spend forty hours a week pounding that message into our children's mind—and then spend millions of dollars researching why youngsters battle anxiety and depression.

Still, even those of us who know the Lord, who love our Bibles, and who have a grasp on our sure and certain hope struggle with anxious hearts. All the factors I've mentioned (and others) contribute to anxiety. We're all different, with various genetics, from various backgrounds, and anxiety is a complex issue. But I think the primary cause of anxiety is simple: we're anxious people because we have a lot to be anxious about. We're spinning on a planet filled with a million dangers. We face scores of daily stresses and distresses, which often come uninvited and unanticipated. We have multiplied fears for our children, our loved ones, our families, our churches, our nation, our world, and ourselves. We have valid concerns about our health and finances, about our safety and our security.

None of us knows what the next day will bring. All of us are subject to debilitating accidents or sudden death at any moment. The pace of life is faster than we can manage, relationships are messy, and the problems of life are greater than we can bear. Parents worry about their children more than anything else, and older parents worry about their adult children even more than younger dads and moms do about their toddlers. Our worries deepen as we age. Life often becomes graver as the grave becomes closer.

Frankly, when I look at the condition of the world, I'm amazed we're not more anxious than we are. And I'm thankful for those who are helping us address these issues genetically, nutritionally, medically, cognitively, and in terms of our lifestyle. I appreciate the doctors, nurses, counselors, therapists, psychologists, psychiatrists, researchers, positive thinkers, pastors, healers, and friends who have helped me through anxious times.

But nothing offers sustained help if we don't have a spiritual foundation based on the Lord Jesus Christ. The core answer to anxiety is a reassuring word from an almighty God. No therapy in the world can match the theology of the Bible. We need help from beyond ourselves and from beyond our worried world. The German humanitarian George Müller spoke for many of us when he said, "Many times when I could have gone insane from worry, I was in peace because my soul believed the truth of [God's] promise."[8]

We have to attack anxiety on the basis of spiritual truth, and I believe that's exactly how Paul dealt with his own issues of worry and stress. Knowing him as we do from the pages of the New Testament, we would expect him to fight his affliction with every available spiritual weapon. Whatever his circumstances, whatever his genetic predispositions, whatever his personality, whatever his background, he was a man who strove toward self-improvement. He worked on his spiritual progress and pressed toward the goal for the prize of the high calling of God. He wanted his whole spirit, soul, and body governed by the Holy Spirit.

As Saint Paul prayerfully searched his books and parchments, pouring over the Hebrew Scriptures, I believe he developed a treatment protocol for his anxiety. He was a strategist, after all, and he crafted a game plan for winning over worry. As a physician of the soul, he knew how to wisely self-medicate with biblical truth.

The day finally came when he was ready to share his method of waging war on worry, and he passed it along to us in the letter of Philippians. Philippians 4:4–9 represents the answer Paul developed for the problem he described in 2 Corinthians 2. He wrote about his crippling anxiety in 2 Corinthians 2:13, sometime around AD 55. Seven or so years later, in about AD 62, he told the Philippians about an eightfold plan for overcoming crippling anxiety.

Here in this memorable passage in Philippians we have Paul's own biblical plan for erasing anxious thoughts and composing our minds with peace in any situation. I believe Philippians 4:4–9 is testimonial in nature. The apostle Paul was sharing with his friends the lessons he had crafted for himself while battling his own interior worlds of worry.

Here is what he wrote:

> Rejoice in the Lord always. I will say it again: Rejoice! Let your gentleness be evident to all. The Lord is near. Do not be anxious about anything, but in every situation, by prayer and petition, with thanksgiving, present your requests to God. And the peace of God, which transcends all understanding, will guard your hearts and your minds in Christ Jesus.
>
> Finally, brothers and sisters, whatever is true, whatever is noble, whatever is right, whatever is pure, whatever is lovely, whatever is admirable—if anything is excellent or praiseworthy—think about such things. Whatever you have learned or received or heard from me, or seen in me—put it into practice. And the God of peace will be with you.

Notice the expansive nature of this advice. It works "in every situation" (verse 6). Notice, too, the instructive phrase near the end of the paragraph in verse 9: "Put it into practice." These verses describe the practices we must develop in overcoming a worried mind in every situation:

- The practice of rejoicing
- The practice of gentleness
- The practice of nearness
- The practice of prayer
- The practice of thanksgiving
- The practice of thinking
- The practice of discipleship
- The practice of peace

The word *practice* implies we must go to work developing certain skills until they become habitual or proficient, like an athlete or musician. These are the Bible's perpetual habits for a gradual and glorious experience with the God of peace. In her book *Better Than Before: What I Learned About Making and Breaking Habits*, Gretchen Rubin called habits "the invisible architecture of daily life. We repeat about 40 percent of our behavior almost daily, so our habits shape our existence, and our future."[9]

Rubin went on to explain that habits reduce the need for self-control, saying, "With habits, we conserve our self-control. Because we're in the habit of putting a dirty coffee cup in the office dishwasher, we don't need self-control to perform that action; we do it without thinking."[10] She also added, "Our habits are our destiny. And changing our habits allows us to alter that destiny."[11]

As it related to his anxiety, it appears Paul made a lot of progress in changing his habits and destiny between the years AD 55 and AD 62, and we can do the same. We may never achieve total immunity from anxiety on earth. Even earlier in the book of Philippians, Paul admitted to jittery nerves over the health of his friend Epaphroditus, who had almost died. He wrote: "I am all the more eager to send him, so that when you see him again you may be glad and I may have less anxiety" (Philippians 2:28).

It may be impossible to avoid worrisome episodes in life, but Paul was determined to have "less anxiety" and to improve his mental health. He wanted to worry less and live more.

His example teaches us we can do better; we can make progress; we can win over worry; and we can move from fretfulness to faithfulness. In the following pages, I invite you to explore Philippians 4:4–9 with me and make this wonderful discovery: while there are good reasons to be worried in today's world, there are *better* reasons not to be. God doesn't want us to be weakened by worry, but fortified by grace.

In one of the Bible's hallowed benedictions, we're given this simple blessing:

> Now may the Lord of peace himself give you peace at all times and in every way. The Lord be with all of you. (2 Thessalonians 3:16)

At all times and in every situation, the Lord of peace Himself wants to give you peace in every way. With that in mind, let's delve into Philippians 4:4–9, verse by verse and line by line, determined to get ourselves into a better place mentally, emotionally, and spiritually—in every situation.

CHAPTER ONE

THE PRACTICE OF REJOICING

Rejoice in the Lord always. I will say it again: Rejoice!

—PHILIPPIANS 4:4

Several years ago, a religious teacher in India named Meher Baba gained a global audience with his odd brand of Eastern mysticism. He claimed to be God in human form and thought of himself as the "avatar of the age," yet he had nothing to say—at least not verbally. He was renowned for his silence. So far as we know, Baba didn't speak a single word for forty years. He communicated using an alphabet board and with hand gestures or by sending cables to his followers. He believed the universe was an illusion, that we're simply figments of the imagination of some higher power. Since nothing is real, he surmised, there is really nothing to trouble us. His most famous saying was short and simple: "Don't Worry. Be Happy." Life is essentially a mirage, he taught, so why worry about it? Have fun while it lasts and just be happy.

In America, Baba's message struck a cord with aging baby boomers and coming-of-age Gen Xers. One of his devotees, Bobby McFerrin, turned Baba's slogan into a popular 1980s song: "Don't Worry Be Happy." McFerrin sang in a breezy style with a playful Caribbean accent and dubbed in the instrumental parts with sounds made with his voice. It became the first a cappella hit to reach Billboard's Hot 100 chart, and it showed up every-where—in presidential campaigns, in films and television shows, in video games, and in performances ranging from musical superstars to middle school glee clubs. It became an unofficial anthem in Jamaica as survivors recovered from the aftermath of Hurricane Gilbert. In the troubled final years of the twentieth century, it conveyed a simple philosophy and a work-able strategy for life in four little words—*don't worry, be happy*.[1]

If only it were that easy!

Imagine! What if a four-word slogan could transport us to a Caribbean beach with no shirt, no shoes, and no problems? What if we could live in a world where Bobby McFerrin met Kenny Chesney, and we all joined in the chorus! If only a mantra could produce a life of cool drinks, lapping waters, tropical breezes, and orange sunsets.

But life isn't an illusion and worry cannot be managed so easily. It takes more than four words of a song. It takes the fourth chapter of Philippians and the solid truths it contains. The slogan "Don't worry, be happy" may express the reality we want, but it provides no roadmap for getting there. It has no compass. It has no doctrine and no theology. It has no foundation in reality. It has pep all right, but no promise.

The Bible says little about being happy, because *happiness* is an emotion that comes and goes depending on happenings. The Bible speaks of some-thing deeper—*joy* and *rejoicing*, which are dispositions of the heart. That's why joy and sorrow are not mutually exclusive. Jesus was anointed with the oil of joy, yet He wept (Hebrews 1:9; John 11:35). The apostle Paul spoke of being sorrowful, yet always rejoicing (2 Corinthians 6:10).

Happiness is an emotion; joy is an attitude. Attitudes are deeper; they are richer; and the right attitudes provide the soil for healthier emotions as we mature. Emotions come and go, but attitudes come and grow. According to Philippians 4:4, the first step toward overcoming anxiety is cultivating the attitude of rejoicing.

It's not *Don't worry; be happy.*

It's *Rejoice in the Lord always. I will say it again: Rejoice!*

It's possible for you to be joyful today. According to the apostle Paul, waging war on worry begins with choosing to tap into the Lord Himself as the fountainhead of hope and as our reservoir of joy. Look at the emphatic nature of Philippians 4:4.

- *Rejoice!*
- Rejoice *in the Lord!*
- Rejoice in the Lord *always!*
- Rejoice in the Lord always; *I will say it again . . .*
- Rejoice in the Lord always; I will say it again—*rejoice!*

Paul repeated the phrase because we need a double dose of it. But what does it actually mean to "rejoice in the Lord always"? After considering this for many years, I've come to see it in four dimensions.

A COMMAND WE OBEY

First, rejoicing is a command to obey. The grammar suggests this, because verse 4 is written as an imperative. It's what God expects us to do. Think again of the apostle Paul's own struggle with anxiety. Based on hints in his writings (like 2 Corinthians 2:12–13), I believe he was a man of nervous energy who battled periodic bouts of stress.

I have a touch of the same affliction, and when I have an attack of nerves nothing helps me more than sitting down with my Bible and searching out verses, promises, and truths from God appropriate to my need at the moment. I assume Paul did the same. Though he had little or none of the New Testament, he had the totality of the Hebrew Scriptures (the Old Testament), which, he said, were "God-breathed" and "useful" (2 Timothy 3:16). We know he poured over the scrolls and the parchments (2 Timothy 4:13), and he told the Romans, "everything that was written in the past was written to teach us, so that through the endurance taught in the Scriptures and the encouragement they provide we might have hope" (Romans 15:4).

Since we know how to go into the Bible and find verses that help us at our points of weakness and need, we can logically assume Paul did the same. Like us, he simply couldn't do without the passages, phrases, verses, truths, promises, and commands of God's Word. I believe his study of the Hebrew Scriptures gave him the phrase he highlighted in Philippians—*rejoice in the Lord.*

This is an Old Testament expression. In fact, except for Paul's quoting it in Philippians 3:1 and 4:4, it's found nowhere in the New Testament. On the other hand, we come across it eleven times in the Old Testament.

Beginning in the book of 1 Samuel and continuing through the prophet Zechariah, we're told to rejoice in the Lord, and the references convey as much authority as the Ten Commandments. When we read the words "Rejoice in the Lord," we can preface them with the words "Thou shalt . . ." This is something God expects, a command to obey. It's a part of obedience and righteousness, and neglecting it is a sin.

Let's quickly trace the eleven-fold use of this phrase in the Old Testament.

- The first person to have uttered the words "Rejoice in the Lord" was Hannah, a woman who had battled extreme anxiety because of severe struggles in her home. But in 1 Samuel 2, the Lord bestowed grace amid her troubles, and, as she worshipped with her little boy, Samuel, in the tabernacle in Shiloh, she exclaimed, "My heart *rejoices in the Lord.*" She had found the secret of converting her pain into praise.
- The next time we see this phrase is from the pen of David, after he repented of devastating sin. He found God's forgiveness, got a new start, brought himself back into the will of the Lord, and exclaimed in Psalm 32:11: "*Rejoice in the Lord and be glad, you righteous; sing, all you who are upright in heart!*"
- We also come across this phrase in Psalm 35, when David was fighting off an attack by his enemies. He prayed for deliverance and pledged to "*rejoice in the Lord and delight in his salvation.*" He declared, "My whole being will exclaim, 'Who is like you, Lord? You rescue the poor from those too strong for them'" (vv. 9–10).

4

- Psalm 64:10 tells us to *rejoice in the Lord*, take refuge in Him, and glory in His name.
- Psalm 97:12 commands, "*Rejoice in the LORD*, you who are righteous, and praise his holy name."
- In Psalm 104:33–34, the writer said, "I will sing to the LORD all my life. . . . May my meditation be pleasing to him, as I *rejoice in the LORD*."
- Isaiah 29:19 says, "Once more the humble will *rejoice in the LORD*; the needy will rejoice in the Holy One of Israel."
- Later on, Isaiah again told his hearers to "*rejoice in the LORD* and glory in the Holy One of Israel" (Isaiah 41:16).
- Joel 2:23 says, "Be glad, people of Zion, *rejoice in the LORD* your God, for he has given you the autumn rains because he is faithful."
- The next occurrence of this phrase comes at the end of the book of Habakkuk, in a passage that represents the most visual depiction of raw faith in God's Word: "Though the fig tree does not bud and there are no grapes on the vines, though the olive crop fails and the fields produce no food, though there are no sheep in the pen and no cattle in the stalls, yet I will *rejoice in the LORD*, I will be joyful in God my Savior" (3:17–18). Even when everything else goes wrong, the Lord Himself stays upright, and we can rejoice in Him.
- The final reference is in Zechariah 10:7, where the Lord promises that the beleaguered Israelites will see better days, be lighthearted, and instinctively obey the injunction of *rejoicing in the Lord*.

In Philippians 4, the apostle Paul reached into his studies of these Scriptures, pulled out this powerful phrase, and used it as the first step in his formula for overcoming worry. This, he felt, was the starting point. This isn't the ending, but it's the beginning of the process of burying worry before worry buries us.

Rejoicing in the Lord demonstrates our willingness to trust God so much that our attitudes are affected. When we make up our minds to rely on Him in storm and sunshine, our burdens are lifted even if our circumstances, for the moment, are unchanged or deteriorating. When we stand on His promises, our spirits are elevated and our emotions lift upward as our perspective shifts Godward. Perhaps your spirits are low right now; mine often are. But it is unhelpful and even unholy to remain in such a condition.

John Wesley, the founder of Methodism, was blessed with a spry and resilient spirit. When a collection of his letters was published, his friend, Samuel Bradburn, wrote an introduction to the volume and used the occasion to describe Wesley's uncanny ability to remain buoyant of spirit:

> I never saw him low-spirited in my life, nor could he endure to be with a melancholy person. When speaking of any who imagined religion would make people morose or gloomy, I have heard him say in the pulpit, that "sour godliness is the devil's religion." In his answer to a letter I had written to him (in a time of strong temptation), he has these words: "(Your) melancholy turn is directly opposite to a Christian spirit. Every believer ought to enjoy life." He never suffered himself to be carried away by extreme grief. I heard him say, "I dare no more fret than curse and swear."[2]

Wesley's natural enthusiasm was buttressed by a firm belief that worry was as wrong as cursing and swearing. He understood Philippians 4:4. Rejoicing isn't just a good idea, a pleasant suggestion, or a laudable quality. God's people are to enjoy life. God wants you to enjoy life, even today. We ought to have joy, and it's not optional. It is a command from the God of all joy who doesn't want His children doubting His providence, distrusting His promises, or discounting His sovereignty.

A CHOICE WE MAKE

That leads to the next dimension of verse 4. Rejoicing in the Lord is not only a command we obey; it's a choice we make. God doesn't give us commandments without providing the grace needed to fulfill them. I've learned the hard way that I must exercise control over my own attitudes.

More accurately, I must let the Holy Spirit have control over them. I don't have to live at the mercy of my feelings. I can choose to smile, to get up off the ground, to cast a heavenward glance, and to decide I'm going to serve the Lord with gladness. Frankly, it's hard to do. I couldn't do it without the truth of Scripture and the grace of God. There comes a time when we say, "I'm tired of living in fear when God has told me to walk by faith and to rejoice in Him always. I'm going to change my outlook to an uplook, even if I have to force myself to adopt a better attitude."

We all battle discouragement. We struggle with anxiety. But with the power of Scripture and the indwelling of the Holy Spirit, we can learn to regulate our personalities. If I'm suddenly overcome with fear about my child's safety at school, I can pause, commit him or her into the Lord's keeping, and remind myself that the Lord is present with my child all the time, and I should rejoice in that right now. Perhaps we can't avoid being cast down, but we don't have to remain in that condition. We can say with the writer of Psalm 42, "Why, my soul, are you downcast? Why so disturbed within me? Put your hope in God" (v. 5). We can't afford the luxury of staying depressed or angry or anxious or fearful. We must acclimatize our minds to a higher plain by learning to rejoice in the Lord.

But notice the prepositional phrase—*in the Lord*. Without it, the verse would be nonsensical. We can't always rejoice in our circumstances. We certainly can't delight in the people or problems that are plaguing us. We can't always rejoice in the state of the world or the status of our homes, marriages, jobs, health, or balance sheets. Those things are a poor basis for joy. But whatever the circumstances, we can always rejoice in our Lord.

That means we rejoice in His *presence*, for in His presence is fullness of joy.

We rejoice in His *precepts* and *promises*, for there is a God-given promise in the Bible to counteract every anxious thought or stressful spot in life. Psalm 19:8 says, "The precepts of the LORD are right, giving joy to the heart."

We can rejoice in His *providence*, for we know that all things work together for good to those who love Him (Romans 8:28).

We can rejoice in His *pardon*, for with His forgiveness comes restoration of His joy. We can rejoice in His *paths* and *purposes* for us. We can rejoice in His *provision*, for our God will supply all our needs (Philippians 4:19).

We can rejoice in His *protection*, for He will never leave us or forsake us. We can rejoice in His *paradise*, for to live is Christ and to die is gain (Philippians 1:21).

In any and every situation, even when we can find few other reasons for happiness, we can rejoice in our Lord and in His attributes and in His infinite fellowship and grace. The best way to generate joy in your life is to cultivate a relationship with Jesus and let Him transform your personality by renewing your thoughts (Romans 12:1–2; 1 Thessalonians 5:16–18).

A CONDITION WE CULTIVATE

Rejoicing in the Lord, then, is a command to obey, a choice to make, and a condition to cultivate. Just as we train a vine to form a topiary, we have to train our minds and our moods to follow the trellis of joy.

When Paul wrote to the Philippians, everything had gone wrong for him. He probably wrote this epistle, as I said, about the year AD 62, in a Roman prison. I don't know if you've been to Italy in the summer, but the heat can be unbearable. In the winter it can dip below freezing. Paul was in an unheated and un–air-conditioned cell, in chains, facing a tense legal challenge for his freedom. He was older and unwell. He had hoped to be engaged in a fourth evangelistic mission; he dreamed of evangelizing Spain. Instead, iron chains rattled whenever he moved, and he had limited sanitation or sustenance.

We might expect him to be anxious. We might think he'd be frustrated or depressed as he wrote to the Philippians. Somewhere in his words, we would expect to hear a tone of self-pity, worry, or grievance. But, no! Philippians is the Epistle of Joy. Recently I read through this little letter with a red pencil and shaded in all the references to joy and rejoicing.

In his opening prayer, he prayed for the Philippians with joy (1:4). He considered his imprisonment to be something God allowed, and he had already seen some benefits from it, saying, "and because of this I rejoice. Yes, and I will continue to rejoice" (1:18).

He wanted to continue ministering to the Philippians for their progress and joy in the faith (1:25), and he longed for them to make him joyful in return (2:2). He was glad and rejoiced in them, and he wanted them to be glad and rejoice with him (2:17–18). He told them to welcome back Epaphroditus with joy (2:29).

In Philippians 3:1, he told them to "rejoice in the Lord," and a chapter later he repeated himself: "Rejoice in the Lord always. I will say it again: Rejoice!" (4:4).

He closed his letter to the Philippians by telling them how he had "rejoiced greatly" because they had sent a financial gift to support his ministry and how he had learned to be content in any and every situation (4:10–11).

The apostle Paul could have interpreted his misfortunes negatively, but he viewed them through the lens of the providence and sovereignty of God, and he chose to sustain a joyful attitude. Because joy was a commandment to obey, he considered it a choice to make, so he cultivated it as the tenor of his soul. He learned to be joyful despite the heat, despite the cold, despite the chains, despite the limitations, despite everything. His attitude was: "Praise the Lord anyway!"

When I was a student at Columbia International University, the faculty and upperclassmen often told stories about one of CIU's graduates, Joy Ridderhof, the head of a missions organization known as Gospel Recordings, Inc. Joy wasn't necessarily joyful by temperament; she was a worrier. But her attitude began to change when she heard a sermon by Dr. Robert C. McQuilkin, who called worry a sin. He said it was "an offense against God as heinous as any crime man can commit."[3]

Joy decided to replace her penchant for worry with a routine of rejoicing, because that seemed a reasonable act of faith in the light of the promises God had given in His Word. She decided on an experiment. Joy sought to deliberately trust God and praise Him for His willingness and ability to bring good out of everything—including her own mistakes. She adopted James 1:2 as her key verse: "Consider it pure joy, my brothers and sisters, whenever you face trials of many kinds."[4]

By a dogged study and application of Bible verses about rejoicing, Joy began to live up to her name and to change the very fabric of her personality. Throughout her life she dealt with loneliness, financial insecurity, ill health, difficult climates, exotic cultures, travel fatigue, and foreign governments, but she stubbornly met each difficulty with a determination to rejoice in the Lord.[5]

In my library, I have a small booklet by Joy Ridderhof that tells of a period of time when, quite suddenly and out of a blue sky, as it were, she relapsed into worry and was overwhelmed with a burden of depression that seemed unbearable. "But from the start," she said, "I set my soul to praise the Lord even more than usual. I sang and rejoiced and the worse it became, the more I expressed praise and worship and thanksgiving to Christ. . . . I . . . knew God, through rejoicing, would be released to do mighty things in my life."

Day after day during this dark period, she chose to sing praises to the Lord, to spend time in thanksgiving, and to rejoice by faith. "As unannounced as it came," she said, "this battle ended and with it such an open door for faith that it seemed as though I could reach out and take the kingdoms for our Lord and Christ."[6]

I don't recall ever meeting Joy Ridderhof. I don't think I ever heard her speak in person. But even hearing others speak about her and her commitment to rejoice had an effect on me as a student. Perhaps it was because of her influence that one of the most popular hymns in our college chapel services was "Rejoice, the Lord Is King," which was written by Charles Wesley, the brother of the aforementioned John.

> *Rejoice the Lord is King,*
> *Your King and Lord adore.*
> *Rejoice, give thanks, and sing,*
> *And triumph evermore.*
> *Lift up your heart,*
> *Lift up your voice,*
> *Rejoice, again I say rejoice!*

A CLIMATE WE CREATE

As that hymn suggests, the joy of the Lord will reset the climate of our souls and our optimism will spread to others. It will be a microclimate we create in our homes, our schools, our workplaces, our churches, and wherever we go. And that's the fourth dimension of Philippians 4:4. Joy is a climate we construct that provides fresh air for those who share our environment.

We have to work on acclimatizing ourselves in this way. For example, I've found it helpful to avoid artificial sadness. I no longer watch sad movies or listen to melancholy music. There is enough sadness in life without generating more of it with sad movies or melancholy music. There are times to weep, to mourn, and to grapple with heartbreak. But God does not want us to remain bogged down in such a state, nor does He want us to foster misery like the paid mourners at ancient funerals. The underlying attitude that serves as the bedrock of our emotions should be the joy of the Lord. We must learn to process our emotions in a way that allows us to continually cycle back to joy.

I'd rather be upbeat than beat up, and I don't want others to be beat up or cast down by my attitude. Our attitudes are as contagious as the plague, and it's important to do for others what Paul was doing for the Philippians. Remember—your attitude is the climate control setting for your marriage, home, school, or workplace.

The Christians in Philippi were worried about Paul and demoralized by his imprisonment. They worried about the future of Christianity. They were anxious. They were discouraged and fearful of persecution. But when Paul wrote to them, his letter conveyed a positive atmosphere. It created a climate of joy in the hearts of the readers.

He told them, "Now I want you to know, brothers and sisters, that what has happened to me has actually served to advance the gospel. . . . through your prayers and God's provision of the Spirit of Jesus Christ what has happened to me will turn out for my deliverance. . . . Whatever happens, conduct yourselves in a manner worthy of the gospel of Christ. . . . for I have learned to be content whatever the circumstances. . . . in any and every situation" (Philippians 1:12, 19, 27; 4:11–12).

Paul's attitude of optimism and peace spread though his contacts in prison, to the Philippians, and on to you and me through his writings. He practiced what he preached—rejoice in the Lord always!—and so can you, in any and every situation.

Katie Hoffman wrote an encouraging book entitled *A Life of Joy*, in which she described her efforts to teach herself to rejoice in the Lord even when things are far from perfect in her circumstances or home:

> From my own experience I know that it's hard to rejoice always, especially when my husband may not be doing what I want him to do. Though I feel like wanting to show him I'm upset by acting downcast, the Holy Spirit still reminds me to rejoice always. I've had to learn, sometimes on my face, that I need to rejoice always no matter what's happening to me or around me. I have had to learn that I can't ever let the actions of other people cause me to sin. I need to be holy before the Lord despite what any other person in all the world does. This is why I emphasize so often how necessary it is for us to keep our minds fixed on things above.
>
> And regardless of how angry or upset I may want to get at a situation, I still have to be filled with love, joy, peace, patience, kindness, goodness, gentleness, faith, and self-control (Galatians 5:22–23). I've also learned from experience that this can be almost impossible if I'm not set on glorifying the Lord Jesus at any and every cost.[7]

When we establish that climate, the sun of righteousness rises with healing in His rays, and every morning brings fresh assurance of God's great faithfulness, mercy, and love. That bolsters our spirits and spans an enthusiastic life.

YOU CAN DO THINGS WITH ENTHUSIASM

Last summer at the Word of Life bookstore in Schroon Lake, New York, I picked up a copy of Harry Bollback's memoirs, and I was hooked from the first page. Harry wrote of growing up in Brooklyn in the 1920s and '30s, and of joining the Marine Corps after graduating from high school in 1943. World War II raged, and Harry was sent to the Pacific. He described his first time in combat, which was on the tiny island of Peleliu. The morning before the battle, Harry found a quiet spot down in the hold of his ship and prayerfully read Psalm 91. As he read it, he came to believe God would preserve him through the war. That was an assurance he badly needed, for his experiences in the South Pacific were horrendous.

"In the battle of Peleliu, in my company of almost 200 men," he wrote, "I was one of only seven who got out without being killed or wounded."[8] He told of his buddies being blown up, of body parts littering the ground around him, of near-death experiences, and of the trauma of war.

Returning home at the end of the conflict, Harry, who was a gifted musician, teamed up with an enthusiastic evangelist named Jack Wyrtzen. They drew thousands of people to huge rallies in New York's Times Square and Madison Square Garden. Wyrtzen was known for his broad smile, powerful preaching, and global vision—and for his ability to extend a gospel invitation that compelled people to come to Christ.

Together, Bollback and Wyrtzen cofounded a ministry called Word of Life. They established camping and conference centers around the world, beginning at beautiful Schroon Lake in upstate New York. Young people streamed to Christ by the thousands at these centers, and the world's best Bible teachers traveled there to minister to vast crowds.

Harry and his wife, Millie, moved to Brazil to establish Word of Life ministries in South America, and Harry's adventures as a missionary in the Amazon rivaled his experiences as a marine in the South Pacific. He ventured by canoe into hostile areas where no man had ever returned alive. Sometimes he dodged arrows; other times he was surrounded by naked tribesmen without knowing their intent. To make a long story short, Harry Bollback established churches in the jungle, camps in the cities, and left a trail of newly redeemed Christians wherever he went.

As I finished Harry's memoirs, I came away wanting to do more for the Lord than ever. The next day, while speaking at a conference at Word of

Life, I recommended the book to the audience, and immediately someone shouted out a whoop of joy. I later learned it was Harry himself, ninety-two years old, who, unknown to me, was in attendance.

The next day Harry invited me to his home, and I spent several hours with him and Millie. I asked him the one question that had perplexed me from his book. Near the end of his memoirs, Harry had written, "The one thing I do wish I could do all over again for the Lord, though, would be to have a little more enthusiasm than I had."[9]

"Harry," I said, "I've seldom read a story of so much energy, passion, adventure, and excitement as yours. Why did you wish you had lived with more enthusiasm?"

"Oh, Jack Wyrtzen!" he replied. "He was the one with enthusiasm! I wish I'd had enthusiasm like Jack's. He could get anything done because of his enthusiasm. He was the most enthusiastic man I've ever known. He showed me that if you have enthusiasm, you can do anything, you can get anything done. I wish I had done everything with a little more enthusiasm!"

I'm with Harry. Looking back on my life, I wish I had done everything with more enthusiasm. Enthusiasm is simply joy translated into daily life. When we rejoice in the Lord always, we're living with enthusiasm, and enthusiasm makes the difference.

The Bible says, "Whatever you do, do it enthusiastically, as something done for the Lord and not for men, knowing that you will receive the reward of an inheritance from the Lord. You serve the Lord Christ" (Colossians 3:23–24 HCSB).

You and I can begin today! Start immediately by memorizing Philippians 4:4 and inscribing it on the walls of your mind. It's easy to learn: "Rejoice in the Lord always. I will say it again: Rejoice!" Repeat it often. Turn it into a song. Adopt it as a slogan. Practice this verse in all its dimensions. Practice it wholeheartedly.

The background music for your life shouldn't be "Don't Worry Be Happy." It should be "Rejoice! The Lord Is King!"

The joy of Jesus isn't optional, but essential, if we're going to erase our anxious thoughts and experience God's irrepressible peace. Rejoicing is a command to obey, a choice to make, a quality to cultivate, and a climate to create for yourself and those around you. It's the first step in worrying less and living more. It's the secret of an enthusiastic life.

> *Rejoice in the Lord always!*
> *I will say it again: Rejoice!*

DISCUSSION QUESTIONS

1. In studying the background of the founding of the church of Philippi in Acts 16, how was joy on display from the very beginning?
2. Why are the words "in the Lord" so important in Philippians 4:4? What divine qualities enable us to rejoice even when there are no figs on the trees or grapes on the vines (Habakkuk 3:17–19)?
3. In what little way can you be more enthusiastic this week?

CHAPTER TWO

THE PRACTICE OF GENTLENESS

Let your gentleness be evident to all.

—PHILIPPIANS 4:5

Richard and Arlene Baughman were married in 1940, just before America entered World War II. Richard was drafted in 1942, and left for the war just a few weeks after the birth of their first son. For more than a year, he was unable to communicate much with his family, and when he returned to his Wisconsin home he bore the scars of posttraumatic stress from combat experiences. He had a lot of bad dreams. But he and Arlene picked up where they left off, and in the years since they have faced everything together. Richard worked as a mail carrier and farmer. Arlene was a schoolteacher. They lived a busy life and raised six children, one of whom passed away. Over the years the Baughmans have encountered all the stresses and strains that come with life, just like you and me.

But here's what sets them apart. Recently this couple celebrated their seventy-fifth anniversary. Richard is now ninety-seven and Arlene is ninety-six years old. Somehow their story got out, and they've been in the news—especially because of an almost unbelievable part of their testimony. In seventy-five years of marriage, they said, they had never had a single argument. Not one. "If we had differences we just talked about it," they said. "We didn't have dishes to throw or shoes to throw because we couldn't afford it. So, we had to get along."[1]

They explained that whenever they felt angry they would give themselves time to cool off before talking it through, and they've always taken time for regular dates and for occasional trips and vacations. They've worked hard, lived simply, not coveted too much, and have tried not to complain to each other. "The couple's advice for a happy marriage," said a reporter who interviewed them, "is to not fret over the small things and to keep faith in the Lord alive."[2]

To me, that's the living embodiment of Philippians 4:5: "Let your gentleness be evident to all." This is the next line of argument the apostle Paul constructed in Philippians 4:4–9 as he relayed his personal strategy for overcoming worry. First, we must make up our minds to rejoice in the Lord in any and every set of circumstances. Second, we must cultivate a gentle spirit. If you want to lower the stresses of life, exhibit a gentler personality and cultivate the art of patience.

WHAT IS GENTLENESS?

When I looked up *gentle* in the dictionary, I was surprised to find the primary definitions were negative. The dictionary talked about what gentleness is not. *Gentleness*, said various dictionaries, means *not* severe, *not* rough, *not* violent. It refers to the *absence of* a bad temper or of belligerence. People who are gentle are *not* harsh, irritable, petulant, or easily offended.

Of course, we can't simply define something by what it's not. It's a positive-sounding word, and we can begin to ferret out a positive definition for gentleness by checking the origin of the English term. The opening syllable—*gen*—comes from the same Latin term that gives us *Genesis, genetics, generation,* and *genital*. It has to do with begetting a family or being part of the same lineage or clan. The word *gentle* originally had to do with the way a mother or father would treat a newborn and with the way we should feel toward those we most love, who are part of our own family.

From its Latin origin, the term passed into the French language, where the Old French version was *gentil*, which meant "born into a good family, highborn, noble." From there it came into our English language as *genteel* ("well-bred, belonging to a polite society"), and *gentle* ("moderate, tender, and kind"). Over time, *gentleness* came to imply softness and kindness, a pleasant demeanor, a naturally sympathetic outlook, and the absence of sharp edges to one's personality. Gentleness suggests a deliberate or voluntary kindness or forbearance in dealing with others. One dictionary said the word *gentleness* involves having a kind nature. Gentle people are amiable, considerate, pleasant, and well tempered.

Paul didn't write to the Philippians in Latin, French, or English. He wrote in Greek, but the Greek term he used (*epieikēs*) has exactly the same meaning as our modern terms. Various English translations of the Bible have rendered this word "considerate," "reasonable," "gentle," and "gracious."

I looked up all twenty-three occurrences of the word *gentle* in the Bible, and based on those references I want to suggest my own definition. When Scripture talks about gentleness it refers to "the ability to stay calm in all our conflicts and kind in all our conduct."

It doesn't mean weakness. It means that in any given situation we've developed the inner resources to remain as calm and kind as is possible under the circumstances. That's one of the greatest assets we can possess. It's a supernatural quality and a spiritual temper of soul. It is Jesus living through us, because we're not like that on our own. This is a biblical quality, and it's vital to developing a Christian personality.

Think of your interactions with your children, your spouse, your coworkers, the clerks behind the counters of coffee shops and discount stores, and even the nuisance callers on the phone. Are you consistently pleasant, calm, and kind?

Yes, there are times to be abrupt and adamant. There are moments to draw a line, to stand up for ourselves, to argue a point, to establish boundaries, and to remain true to what's right. Yet we should always do so as gently as possible in any given circumstance. There is never a moment when we should be one degree harsher than we must. We should always be as gentle as possible, and our gentleness should manifest itself in our eyes, in our facial expression, in our body posture, in the tone of our voices, and in our subsequent actions.

As I tracked down and studied the occurrences of the word *gentle* in the Bible, I came away with four great benefits that come into the lives of gentle people.

REDUCES ANXIETY

First, a gentle spirit reduces anxiety, which is Paul's point in Philippians 4. When you read between the lines of this epistle, you get the idea that some of the personalities in the Philippian church had rough edges. This church, as we know from the New Testament, was exemplary, but it wasn't perfect. Apparently, some of the pews were occupied by people who had sharp angles to their temperaments. Throughout Paul's short letter to them, we pick up clues.

- In chapter 1, Paul's primary prayer for the Philippians was for their love to "abound more and more in knowledge and depth of insight" (Philippians 1:9).
- He told them, "Whatever happens, conduct yourselves in a manner worthy of the gospel of Christ. Then, whether I come and see you or only hear about you in my absence, I will know that you stand firm in one Spirit . . . together as one" (Philippians 1:27).
- In chapter 2, the apostle pled with the Philippians to be "like-minded, having the same love, being one in spirit and of one mind." He told them, "Do nothing out of selfish ambition or vain conceit. Rather, in humility value others above yourselves, not looking to your own interests but each of you to the interests of others" (Philippians 2:2–4).
- He said, "In your relationships with one another, have the same mindset as Christ Jesus" (Philippians 2:5). He went on to describe the remarkable condescension and gentleness of the Lord Jesus, who "humbled himself by becoming obedient to death" (Philippians 2:8).

- On the basis of Christ's example, then, Paul told them, "Do everything without grumbling or arguing" (Philippians 2:14).
- In the latter part of Philippians 2, Paul described two men whose gentleness and encouragement had changed his life—Timothy and Epaphroditus (Philippians 2:19–30).
- In the opening verses of chapter 4, Paul took the unusual step of addressing two women by name, Euodia and Syntyche. He urged them to drop their feud, and he asked a mutual friend to help them.
- And in Philippians 4:5–6, Paul indicated we should learn to be gentle so we don't create needless anxiety for ourselves or for others.

It's easy to be like the mother of my friend Keith Fletcher. As she grew older, she became increasingly cantankerous, difficult, and critical. Her sharp comments made her a bit of a challenge to live with. A couple of months after she passed away, Keith had a dream about her. He dreamed he came downstairs for supper and there she was sitting at the table, the same as always.

"Mom! You're here!" Keith exclaimed. "You're back."

She nodded.

He said, "But you passed away and went to heaven."

She nodded again.

"Mom, if you've been to heaven, you've seen it there and you know what it's like. You can tell us all about heaven. What is it like there? What is heaven really like?"

She shot a glance at him and said curtly, "I didn't like it!"

The question isn't whether we know people like that. It's whether we're like that ourselves more often than we realize. Keith's mother reflects our own natural tendencies. Just last week while reading in the book of Numbers during my morning devotions, I was struck by the critical attitudes of the children of Israel in the desert. Their constant complaining resembled smokestacks billowing out smog at full blast, and I grew convicted about my own tendency to grumble and whine about my workload, my fatigue, my busyness, my aches and pains, and all the rest of it.

Gentle people learn to temper their attitudes with a pleasant, patient approach that's quietly adjusted and recalibrated every day during our devotions. In his book *Breakfast with Fred*, management consultant Fred Smith told of his friend Ron Glosser, who was the head of the Hershey Trust Company in Hershey, Pennsylvania. Glosser said that when he found himself being overly critical, the problem was likely to be in his own heart rather than in the other person's behavior. Glosser realized he needed a way to keep his thinking healthy. He said, "I have found that the best way to keep from being overly critical is to get myself centered early in the day. For me, this is achieved by reading the Scriptures and praying. I try to identify myself as the beloved child of God and to see all those with whom I come in contact that same way."[3]

When we fail to do this, we face needless tension. Some people keep everyone torn up. They are always involved in conflict and raise stress levels wherever they go. Difficult or demanding people put a lot of pressure on themselves and others. The Bible is full of examples of those whose lives were complicated by a stern or stubborn demeanor.

- In 1 Samuel 25, a wealthy farmer named Nabal had the reputation of being surly and rude in his dealings. He got into an altercation with David and his men, and he ended up having a stroke and dying.
- In 1 Kings 12, King Rehoboam entertained a delegation of countrymen asking him to relax governmental policies. Rehoboam consulted his older advisers, who counseled him to listen to the people and respond with gentleness and favor. The king then sought the advice of the buddies he had grown up with, and they suggested a harsh approach. The king took a rigid stand against his people. As a result, he lost ten of the twelve tribes that made up his kingdom. The nation of Israel split apart like a ripped sheet and was never reunified.
- In the New Testament, Paul dealt with many difficult people, and on one occasion he warned Titus about being drawn into conflicts with such people. He said, "Warn a divisive person once, and then warn them a second time. After that, have nothing to do with them. You

may be sure that such people are warped and sinful; they are self-condemned" (Titus 3:10–11).

This, then, is the tenor of Philippians 4. Paul's endorsement of a gentle approach to others is based on a simple observation. Some people create anxiety for themselves and for others by disagreeableness, by their sharp tongues, by their opinionated personalities, and by their irritable spirits. When you're upset, you upset others, which piles on layers of stress like wet blankets. If you're angry at home, you'll upset your marriage. If you're harsh at work, you'll have more conflicts.

To reduce anxiety, then, develop a gentle spirit.

In one of her uplifting poems, Helen Steiner Rice put it like this:

> At the spot God placed you
> Begin at once to do
> Little things that brighten up
> The lives surrounding you.
> For if everybody brightened up
> The spot on which they're standing
> By being more considerate
> And a little less demanding
> This dark old world would very soon
> Eclipse the "Evening Star"
> If everybody brightened up
> The corner where they are.[4]

REFLECTS CHRIST

A gentle spirit not only reduces anxiety; it also reflects Christ. In Matthew 11:29, Jesus spoke of Himself as "gentle and humble in heart," and in Matthew 21:5, others described Him as being "gentle and riding on a . . . colt."

This didn't keep Jesus from speaking plainly when necessary. There were times He condemned hypocrites, denounced cities, and rebuked demons. He occasionally spoke sharply (Matthew 16:23), and just a reproachful glance could reduce a grown man to tears (Luke 22:61–62). But there was never a time when Jesus lost control of Himself or of His words or emotions. The default setting on His personality was one of compassion, love, gentleness, and humility—a willingness to touch and help those with whom He came in contact.

I have a small ornamental pond along the front corner of my house, and a couple of months ago I purchased two small fish—koi. I paid six or seven dollars each for them, and they've grown very quickly. But they're so skittish we have trouble seeing them. From a distance we'll see them swimming around in their little world, but as soon as we approach, they panic. They dart back and forth as if we were going to kill and eat them, desperately looking for a rock or lily pad to hide behind. I've been reading articles about how to tame koi, but so far we've not established fellowship.

That resembles how we sometimes feel toward God. He rises up, towers over us, and gazes down into our little pond, and we're afraid of Him. He is vast, unbounded, absolute in all His attributes and holy in all His ways. In one respect, the proper fear of the Lord represents a healthy attitude of reverence and awe. But our Lord is also a loving God, and He did the unimaginable by jumping into the pond with us, as it were. When we see Jesus, we see the gentleness and the tenderness and the compassion of God, and according to Hosea 11:4, the Lord draws us to Himself with "gentle cords, with bands of love" (NKJV).

Sometimes when I feel particularly sinful or unworthy, I think of the verse that is spoken about Christ in both the Old and the New Testaments: "A bruised reed he will not break, and a smoldering wick he will not snuff out" (Isaiah 42:3; Matthew 12:20).

God loves you and me greatly and gently, and through Jesus Christ, He reaches out to us with all the tenderness of His nail-scarred hands. When we respond to His love and receive Him as Lord and Savior, He moves into our hearts and begins to remodel our temperaments. He permeates our personalities with nine different attitudes, which reflect His own character.

These are called the "fruit of the Spirit," and one of them is gentleness. Galatians 5:19–23 says, "The acts of the flesh are obvious . . . hatred, discord, jealously, fits of rage, selfish ambition, dissensions, factions. . . . But the fruit of the Spirit is love, joy, peace, forbearance, kindness, goodness, faithfulness, gentleness, and self-control."

Notice quality number eight: gentleness.

Another passage along the same lines, Ephesians 4:1–2, says, "live a life worthy of the calling you have received. Be completely humble and gentle." In other words, when we are completely humble and completely gentle, we demonstrate a life worthy of the calling we have received.

Husbands and wives need to remember this in their marriages, and parents need to practice this with their children. Brothers and sisters need to remember this. Many of our most anxious or stressful moments occur within family relationships, often under the same roof. We feel neglected or affronted. We get angry. We argue. We speak harshly. We insult. We yell or scream. We lose our temper and our compassion. We sulk and withdraw our love. None of that reflects the personality of the Lord Jesus Christ.

In her book *I Never Walk the Halls Alone*, Donna Kincheloe wrote about her experiences as a critical care nurse. One of her most touching memories involved her grandfather, who had raised her. When she received word of his heart attack, she raced to his side in a Pennsylvania hospital, where she found him unable to speak. He tried desperately to communicate, but he couldn't vocalize his words. Through long experience in intensive care units, Donna had learned to read lips and she quickly realized her grandfather was pleading to see his two children, Dee and Bud. Years before, these two siblings had argued and grown embittered toward each other. They had not spoken for a dozen years. Now they met at their dying father's bedside.

"My mom and Uncle Bud wanted me there to interpret, so, next visiting time, the three of us went to Grandpa's bedside," Donna recalled. "Mom was on his left and Uncle Bud was on his right. Grandpa reached up and took Mom's right hand and Bud's left hand and put them together. He then covered their hands with his own strong mechanic's hands and mouthed two words over and over, 'Make up. Make up. Make up.'"[5]

Donna went on to suggest that Jesus, by His death, had a similar objective. He wants to reunite us with our heavenly Father and with each other, and His wounded hands can bring healing to our relationships and replace hostility with gentleness and understanding.[6]

That was Paul's message in Philippians 4, when he told Euodia and Syntyche to make up. He called on others to help the women through the process of healing, and he told the whole church to practice gentleness: "Let your gentleness be evident to all."

> Therefore, as God's chosen people, holy and dearly loved, clothe yourselves with compassion, kindness, humility, gentleness and patience. Bear with each other and forgive one another if any of you has a grievance against someone. Forgive as the Lord forgave you. And over all these virtues put on love, which binds them all together in perfect unity.
>
> Let the peace of Christ rule in your hearts, since as members of one body you were called to peace. And be thankful. (Colossians 3:12–15)

GETS THINGS DONE

As I studied the occurrences of the words *gentle* and *gentleness* in the Bible, I also ran into a pragmatic truth. The Bible says we should be gentle because gentleness gets things done. It works. It makes us more efficient, productive, and profitable in the daily business of life. Gentleness not only reduces stress and reflects Christ, it simply gets things done.

There are two verses about this in the book of Proverbs. The first is Proverbs 25:15: "Through patience a ruler can be persuaded, and a gentle tongue can break a bone." One of the softest parts of our body is the tongue. God created it with flexibility and motion so we can eat and speak. The most unyielding parts of our body are our bones, which are so rigid we can stand upright. But according to Proverbs 25:15, a gentle tongue is stronger than a rigid bone. We could paraphrase this verse to say that a person who knows how to speak gently will be more effective in any situation than someone who is rigid and severe. The New Century Version says, "A gentle word can get through to the hard-headed."

I learned this lesson when I was in high school and working at Jim Chambers Men's Shop in my hometown of Elizabethton, Tennessee. Jim was a wonderful man, a Christian, and he'd been a retailer for many years with a loyal base of customers in our community. One day while I was working in the back of the store, a man—a farmer and a hillbilly—burst into the store like a thunderclap. He was upset over a pair of shoes he had purchased. He let Jim have it, telling him how sorry the shoes were, how they hurt his feet, how they didn't fit right, how they weren't made well, how he'd been cheated. There in front of Jim and the other customers, he flew into a fit. My heart stopped and I felt a panic attack coming on. Jim just stood there, looking at the man and at the shoes and nodding thoughtfully during the rant.

When the man finished, I waited for my boss to let him have it back. But Jim just said, "Mr. Farmer, I'm sorry you don't like your shoes. Sometimes we just get a bad pair, don't we? What would you like me to do about it? Would you like your money back? Would you like another pair of shoes? I'll be glad to give you another pair. You just pick them out. Here, I'll throw in a pair of socks."

The farmer just wilted. He looked down, his anger spent, and he said, "Well, I guess another pair of shoes would be all right, Jim."

Jim looked at me and said, "Robert, help this man find another pair of shoes." I guess Jim didn't know I panicked in confrontation, and my hands were shaking a bit as I pulled boxes off the shelves. But I got the farmer shod, and as soon as he was out the door, Jim smiled at me and said, "I lost a pair of shoes but I kept a customer."

That leads to the other great verse about this in Proverbs, one of the most psychologically sound verses of Scripture—Proverbs 15:1: "A gentle answer turns away wrath, but a harsh word stirs up anger." That's a verse to post to the bulletin board of your memory. It's a sentence to teach our children as soon as they're old enough to memorize it. It's only thirteen words, and most are one syllable. But no verse in the Bible conveys better psychology.

Proverbs 15:1 also seeps into many other New Testament passages, which advise leaders to master the art of the gentle answer. Influencers must know how to put these truths into action. The apostle Paul instructed Timothy to appoint church overseers who were "not violent but gentle, not quarrelsome" (1 Timothy 3:3).

A bit later, Paul added, "Do not rebuke an older man harshly, but exhort him as if he were your father. Treat younger men as brothers, older women as mothers, and younger women as sisters" (1 Timothy 5:1–2). He went on to tell him to cultivate certain leadership traits in his personality, including "righteousness, godliness, faith, love, endurance and gentleness" (1 Timothy 6:11).

A few pages later, Paul instructed another protégé, Titus, to be "gentle toward everyone" and to teach all the church members to be the same (Titus 3:2).

The apostle Peter told us to adopt the same strategy, even with unbelievers who don't know Christ. "But in your hearts revere Christ as Lord," wrote Peter. "Always be prepared to give an answer to everyone who asks you to give the reason for the hope that you have. But do this with gentleness and respect" (1 Peter 3:15).

Successful people cultivate the quality of gentleness, which means reining in the rougher elements of their tempers and practicing self-control with their tongues. They have learned to be calm in all their conflict and kind in all their conduct.

With a little thought, we can devise personal techniques that allow our gentleness to show through. One man did it by holding a pipe in his hand. Harold Wilson served two stints as Britain's prime minister in the 1960s and '70s. He was frequently seen with a pipe in his hand, though he preferred cigars. He ended up with that pipe in his hand because he had a bad habit of raising his hand as a fist when making a point, especially during television interviews. His advisor, Marcia Williams, felt this looked threatening to viewers, so she gave him a pipe to hold as a prop. It worked, and Wilson exuded a gentler and more confident appearance, leading to his political success.[7]

Rocky Forshey of Houston, Texas, told me that years ago when his children were young he would grow upset at them and tramp through the house to scold them. Passing a mirror once, he was shocked at the fierce countenance on his face. He realized that's how his children saw him. He instantly softened his face, and he took the lesson to heart. He began practicing relaxing his expression whenever he spoke with his children, and it became a lifelong habit that has given Rocky a countenance that isn't rocky at all, but gentle and wise.[8]

John Wooden, one of the most revered coaches in the history of college basketball, credited much of his success to his dad. He recalled a boyhood occasion when he watched his father deal with a certain situation. His rural Indiana county would pay local farmers to take teams of mules or horses into the gravel pits scattered through the county and haul out loads of gravel. Some pits were deeper than others, and sometimes it was hard for a team to pull a wagon filled with gravel out through the wet sand and up the steep incline.

One steamy summer day, wrote Wooden, a young farmer was trying to get his team of horses to pull a fully loaded wagon out of the pit. He was whipping and cursing those beautiful plow horses, which were frothing at the mouth, stomping, and pulling back from him. The elder Wooden watched for a while, then went over to the young man and said, "Let me take 'em for you."

Dad started talking to the horses, almost whispering to them, and stroking their noses with a soft touch. Then he walked between them, holding their bridles and bits while he continued talking—very calmly and gently—as they settled down. Gradually he stepped out in front of them and gave a little whistle to start them moving forward while he guided the reigns. Within moments, those two big plow horses pulled the wagon out of the gravel pit as easy as could be. As if they were happy to do it.[9]

John Wooden said, "I've never forgotten what I saw him do and how he did it. Over the years I've seen a lot of leaders act like that angry young farmer who lost control. . . . So much more can usually be accomplished by Dad's calm, confident, and steady approach."[10]

Wooden took away an indelible lesson: "It takes strength inside to be gentle on the outside."[11]

Gentleness does not imply weakness; it conveys strength, maturity, self-control, and a desire to be productive in life. It requires a strong self-image. Insecure people get their dander up. They feel threatened. They feel slighted and offended, and they compensate by overreacting. As we mature in Christ, we exchange our low image of ourselves with a high image of Christ. The Holy Spirit forms His personality within us and teaches us the incredible power of a gentle spirit.

PLEASES THE LORD

And that pleases the Lord, which brings me to my final thought. A gentle spirit reduces anxiety, reflects Christ, gets things done, and, most importantly, pleases the Lord. He is delighted when we are gentle, and He is grieved when we aren't. There's a wonderful verse about this in the Bible. It was originally addressed to women, but its message is transferable to all of us.

> Your beauty should not come from outward adornment, such as elaborate hairstyles and the wearing of gold jewelry or fine clothes. Rather, it should be that of your inner self, the unfading beauty of a gentle and quiet spirit, which is of great worth in God's sight. (1 Peter 3:3–4)

Look at those words: "a gentle . . . spirit, which is of great worth in God's sight." According to the apostle Peter, this is true elegance, and it's the way we make ourselves appealing to others, to the world, and to the Lord. When I was a boy, my parents, both schoolteachers, sometimes took me to Knoxville, Tennessee, for their educational conferences, and we always stayed downtown at the Farragut Hotel, next door to the S&W

Cafeteria. One year my elderly grandparents accompanied us, and during supper my grandfather, Clifton Palmer, grew agitated. Turning to my mom, he said, "An old man across the room keeps scowling at me." We all looked, of course. The opposite wall was lined with mirrors, and my grandfather had been looking at no one but himself.

If only we could see the expression on our faces the way others see us!

If you want a more attractive face, learn to be gentle, quiet, and confident in your demeanor. Ecclesiastes 8:1 says, "A person's wisdom brightens their face and changes its hard appearance." Gentleness is the world's most exclusive beauty secret. If only we could bottle it! It relaxes our faces and releases our smiles. It pleases God.

There's scant gentleness in our world. Just turn on the radio or television. Watch a movie. Read blog comments or social media posts. People are indignant. People are shouting at each other. People insult one another in our increasingly coarse culture. This demanding spirit can seep into our homes and churches. I confess I'm not as gentle as I should be in reacting to provocation or fatigue or stress. But as Christians we should be keen to improve. When we trust Jesus Christ as our Lord and Savior, we begin to change and we keep improving as long as we're on earth. And a gentle spirit reduces our stress, reflects Christ, gets things done, and pleases the Lord.

Remember what Saint Francis de Sales said: "Nothing is so strong as gentleness, nothing so gentle as real strength."[12] A good place to start is by memorizing and practicing Philippians 4:5: *Let your gentleness be evident to all.*

DISCUSSION QUESTIONS

1. Why did the Lord insert the words, "Let your gentleness be evident to all," in the middle of the Bible's premier passage about worry and anxiety?
2. Is gentleness a characteristic of strength or weakness? What more

can we learn about gentleness from Proverbs 15:1? Matthew 11:29? Galatians 5:22–23? First Peter 3:15?

3. In your own experience, who has displayed an attitude of gentleness that has touched your life? In what way do you need to exhibit a gentler spirit?

CHAPTER THREE

THE PRACTICE OF NEARNESS

The Lord is near.

—PHILIPPIANS 4:5

During my college days, a few buddies and I were hiking somewhere in a beautiful gorge when we detoured over a ravine by walking across a fallen tree. I was halfway across the thing when I froze up and got tottery. The ground seemed as if it was a mile below me. I recall flailing my arms like a windmill and shouting, "I've lost my nerve!" The friend in front of me instantly reached out and took hold of my hand. I could have pulled us both off the log, but somehow the momentary touch of my friend's hand gave stability. I regained my balance and made it safely to the other side.

I've thought of that many times when I've gotten weak-kneed over other chasms, and it's the touch of a Friend's hand that has steadied me. The same is true for the heroes of Scripture. When Peter sank in alarm trying to walk across the choppy waters of Galilee, Jesus immediately reached out His hand and caught him, saying, "You of little faith . . . why did you doubt?" (Matthew 14:31).

Many of the Psalms speak of the nearness of God's hand:

- "I keep my eyes always on the LORD. With him at my right hand, I will not be shaken" (Psalm 16:8).

- "Your right hand sustains me" (Psalm 18:35).
- "I cling to you; your right hand upholds me" (Psalm 63:8).
- "Your hand is strong" (Psalm 89:13).
- "You will fill me with joy in your presence, with eternal pleasures at your right hand" (Psalm 16:11).

One of my favorite promises in Scripture—I found and memorized this verse in childhood—says:

> So do not fear, for I am with you;
>> do not be dismayed, for I am your God.
> I will strengthen you and help you;
>> I will uphold you with my righteous right hand. (Isaiah 41:10)

When you spot a couple walking down the street hand-in-hand, you know they're in love. The same is true for us in our love for Jesus. We enjoy the Lord's fellowship when holding His unchanging hand, and as we cultivate a sense of His nearness, we grow increasingly intimate with Him. We're strengthened and steadied by the nearness of His touch.

The stresses of life rattle our minds. We feel tottery and worry about falling off the log. As we've seen, this even happened to Paul in Troas when he couldn't complete his mission. But the apostle worked through these issues and later penned the Bible's greatest passage against worry. His eight-point strategy in Philippians 4 begins with the practices of rejoicing and gentleness. Then it goes on to suggest we cultivate the practice of nearness. Verse 5 ends with the words: *The Lord is near.*

I have my Bible open to Philippians 4 as I'm writing this, and it occurs to me the passage would have continued smoothly had these words been omitted. The Lord could have left them out of His Scripture and we wouldn't have known the difference: *Rejoice in the Lord always. I will say it again: Rejoice! Let your gentleness be evident to all. Do not be anxious about anything.*

But, oh, how vital those four words: *The Lord is near.* How great our loss had they been left out!

Yet this is the most difficult sentence to interpret in the entire paragraph. What did Paul mean by saying the Lord is near? That question has perplexed translators and commentators for two thousand years. Was Paul referring to time or to space or to both? If the first, Paul meant, "The Lord's coming is near." If the second, he meant, "The Lord's presence is near." If both, he meant, "Jesus is near, and that's true in two ways. He is near you presently, and His coming isn't far away either."

This dilemma is reflected in the various translations we use. Compare these two renderings from popular versions of the Bible:

- The Lord is ever present with us (THE VOICE).
- The Lord is coming soon (NLT).

Since Paul was a literary and theological genius who knew when a phrase could have a double meaning, and since both interpretations reflect unquestioned scriptural truth, I'm going to assume Paul meant: "The Lord is near to us—period—both in terms of His coming and in terms of His presence, so do not worry about anything."

Let me show you how this works out.

THE LORD'S COMING IS NEAR

In the New Testament, the word *near* was sometimes used in connection with the return of Jesus Christ to earth, and several commentaries suggest this was on Paul's mind as he wrote Philippians 4:5.

In Matthew 24, for example, Jesus listed the "signs of the times" that would herald the nearness of His return, then He said, "Even so, when you see all these things, you know that it [My coming] is near, right at the door" (v. 33).

James added, "You too, be patient and stand firm, because the Lord's coming is near" (James 5:8).

Peter said, "The end of all things is near. Therefore be alert and of sober mind so that you may pray" (1 Peter 4:7).

The book of Revelation begins and ends by declaring our Lord's coming is near at hand (Revelation 1:3 and 22:10).

You may ask, "Those words were written nearly two thousand years ago, and Jesus still hasn't come. That doesn't seem like 'near' to me. If believers in New Testament days thought Jesus would return any moment, but He didn't come as they expected, why should we still be looking for Him now?"

Great question.

First, the Bible was written from God's perspective, and His concept of *nearness* is different from ours. To God, the time between our Lord's first and second comings is just a moment. From the vantage point of eternity, it's just a day or two. Peter pointed this out to critics in the first century who were impatient for the Lord's return and who demanded, "Where is this 'coming' he promised?" (2 Peter 3:4).

Peter replied, "Do not forget this one thing, dear friends: With the Lord a day is like a thousand years, and a thousand years are like a day. The Lord is not slow in keeping his promise, as some understand slowness" (vv. 8–9).

To our everlasting God, a thousand years resemble the passing of a single day. From the vantage of eternity, then, Jesus has only been gone from earth a couple of days. He understands nearness and slowness from a different frame of reference. We dwell in time, but we share Christ's everlasting life. Believers in every generation have expected Jesus to come in their lifetimes, which is how it should be. The Lord wants us to live with anticipation and readiness, and, from His perspective, we may well be down to the last hours or minutes. His coming is soon, as He understands soonness, and that's good enough for me.

Second, there is a potentially more immediate nearness to our reunion with the Savior. If He doesn't come to us during our lifetimes, we will go to be with Him at the end of our lifetimes, and that could happen at any second. None of us has the promise of tomorrow. Every human on our planet is subject to sudden death at any moment, and Christians are not excluded. The possibility of our being reunited with our Lord is imminent, either through His sudden coming to us or through our departure to be with Him.

Sometimes when I'm overwhelmed with worry or with the weight of my problems, I remind myself that fifty years from now, I'll not be worried about any of this (unless I still manage to be alive at 115). When the Lord takes His children out of the world, they're released from all their problems, and this provides great solace. Jesus told the thief on the cross beside Him, "Truly I tell you, today you will be with me in paradise" (Luke 23:43).

One of the things we most look forward to about heaven is freedom from every worry, anxiety, and care. Revelation 21:4 says, "'He will wipe every tear from their eyes. There will be no more death, or mourning or crying or pain, for the old order of things has passed away.'"

We're presently part of the old order of things. We've living under a curse that fell across the universe because of sin. But for Christ-followers, our problems are temporary and our burdens are momentary, but our blessings are permanent. Whatever we're worrying about now will be of no concern to us a hundred years from now. God will release us from all our troubles and work them all for our good. He'll take over our problems and resolve them for His glory, and we can rest in a glorious future. The hymnist said:

> Not now, but in the coming years,
> It may be in the better land,
> We'll read the meaning of our tears,
> And there, some time, we'll understand.[1]

Two great verses of the Bible make this point:

- "I consider that our present sufferings are not worth comparing with the glory that will be revealed in us" (Romans 8:18).
- "For our light and momentary troubles are achieving for us an eternal glory that far outweighs them all" (2 Corinthians 4:17).

These are remarkable verses to ponder. Compared to the endless joys and untroubled life we're anticipating in heaven, our worst problems are, from that perspective, "light and momentary" and "not worth comparing with the glory that will be revealed."

This mind-set infuses Philippians 4:5 with meaning, and, indeed, it illumines the whole atmosphere of Philippians. The apostle Paul began the book with his great personal statement of purpose: "For to me, to live is Christ and to die is gain. If I am to go on living in the body, this will mean fruitful labor for me. Yet what shall I choose? I do not know! I am torn between the two: I desire to depart and be with Christ, which is better by far; but it is more necessary for you that I remain in the body" (Philippians 1:21–24).

In other words, Paul relished the prospects of going to heaven, leaving behind all his stresses and strains and pains. He was eager to be rid of his worries and to be with the Lord, which would be better for him by far. Yet he felt God still had some remaining fruitful labor for him on this planet, so he was willing to stay earthbound awhile longer.

Later, in Philippians 3, in discussing his adversaries, Paul wrote:

> For, as I have often told you before and now tell you again even with tears, many live as enemies of the cross of Christ. Their destiny is destruction, their god is their stomach, and their glory is in their shame. Their mind is set on earthly things. But our citizenship is in heaven. And we eagerly await a Savior from there, the Lord Jesus Christ, who, by the power that enables him to bring everything under his control, will transform our lowly bodies so that they will be like his glorious body. (Philippians 3:18–21)

When I was a little boy, ten or eleven years old, my dad promised to take us to Myrtle Beach, South Carolina, on vacation. We'd been there before, and I can't tell you how excited I was. I loved going to Myrtle Beach, chowing down on pancakes in the morning, playing in the ocean all day, riding everything at the carnival in the evening, playing miniature golf, and having my parents' full attention for the whole week.

My little sister, Ann, was about five, and I wanted her to be as excited about the trip as I was. I wrote to the Myrtle Beach Chamber of Commerce asking for brochures. A week or so later, I began getting brochures by the dozens from every attraction, amusement park, hotel, restaurant, and golf course on the Grand Strand. I organized them on a folding table and went over every brochure with Ann. I had her so excited she could hardly sleep at night. We were so wound up with anticipation we almost could have flown there by flapping our arms.

In the week before we left, I might have gotten into trouble with my parents. One of those lost library books might have plagued me. Maybe I had a flat tire on my bicycle. I probably scraped my knee. But I recovered from all such problems more quickly because I was busy packing for the beach. The anticipation of the trip eclipsed everything else in my life.

I still love going to Myrtle Beach, and I get great joy anticipating other trips as well. But there's one destination I'm looking forward to above all. In times of anxiety or distress I remind myself, "None of these problems are going to matter to me in a few years. All my worries are short-lived, and in any event God has promised they will somehow turn out for good."

Abraham lived in tents and weathered the troubles of life by faith, "for he was looking forward to the city with foundations, whose architect and building is God . . . longing for a better country—a heavenly one" (Hebrews 11:10, 16).

Can you see how eternal anticipation is an antidote to current frustration? The regular contemplation of the Lord's return and of heaven is an essential biblical therapy for worry. The Bible is all about the future. Page after page and passage after passage is devoted to prophecy, to what's ahead, to the resurrection, to the return of Christ, to the endless adventures of everlasting life.

The next time you fall into an anxious state, take a deep breath, put your problem on hold, find a quiet spot, and read Revelation 21–22, which is the Bible's travel brochure of heaven. Picture the diamond city of New Jerusalem descending like a jewel to the New Earth. Visualize the streets, walls, gates, throne, and crystal river. Read 1 Thessalonians 4 about the moment of Christ's return. Study prophecy. See what the Bible says about the future. Our burdens cannot follow us to heaven, and our trials and troubles are not worth comparing to the glory that will be revealed in us.

The Message renders Philippians 4:5–6 this way: "the Master is about to arrive. He could show up any minute! Don't fret or worry."

THE LORD'S PRESENCE IS NEAR

The other application of the phrase "The Lord is near" in Philippians 4:5, has to do with physical proximity. The Lord is close beside you right now, so don't worry about things; instead, pray about them. Almighty God is here, in our geographical zone, closer than we realize, now, accompanying us, surrounding us, sharing our space, even living within us. He is an ever-present help in trouble (Psalm 46:1).

It's plain to see how this reality would lessen our quotient of worry. When we consider the nearness of Christ, we're reminded that He walks beside us every moment. He notices the look in our eyes, the tone in our voice, the catch in our heart, and the sigh on our lips. And He longs for His very presence to calm and control us.

Paul learned this from experience in Acts 21–23, when he encountered a series of disastrous events. After inadvertently sparking a riot in the Jewish temple, he was nearly killed by a mob, only to be rescued by Roman soldiers who stripped him and strung him up by the wrists to be flogged. He talked his way out of that ordeal, but then he was dragged before the city council to defend himself. His plans and prospects wilted under the threat of prolonged imprisonment, crippling legal threats, and likely execution.

Put yourself in his place—a disrupted life bound up in legal challenges, probable imprisonment, and waves of financial and physical strain.

But at that perilous moment Paul had a jailhouse visitor whose presence changed everything. Acts 23:11 says, "The following night the Lord stood near Paul and said, 'Take courage! As you have testified about me in Jerusalem, so you must also testify in Rome.'"

Notice those words, "The Lord *stood near* Paul and said . . ." Those words imply some sort of physical reality, an actual presence there behind prison walls, standing beside Paul as truly as a human personage. The word *Lord* is typically the way the New Testament writers designated Jesus Christ. This near-at-hand Lord spoke with commanding reassurance, saying: "Take courage! As you have testified about me in Jerusalem, so you must also testify in Rome."

When you turn to Jesus, He comes, stands beside you, is actually present by His Spirit, speaks through His Word, wards off fear, imparts courage, and reassures you about His promises and plans. That's what Paul experienced in Acts 23:11; in Philippians 4:5–6 he passed the lesson on to us: "The Lord is ever present with us. Don't be anxious about things; instead, pray" (THE VOICE).

It's true that God is everywhere at once, omnipresent, in every location of every realm in the visible and invisible spheres. God is not measurable, and the essence of His personality fills the galaxies and extends beyond the limits of the universe, traversing all the territories of fathomless infinity. He occupies every address, inhabits every sector, tracks every vector, and resides in every corner of the universe. He fills heaven and earth.

Yet in a personal way, our Lord draws near and speaks to us in times of stress, worry, anxiety, or fear. As I look back over my adult life, I've had a lot of times when I've been overtaken with anxiety. I've had times when I almost suffocated with worry. But what I remember most about those times is how they drove me to sit down, open my Bible, cry out to the Lord, pray to Him, and find specific Bible verses that calmed me down and gave me strength and courage. Those have become my favorite verses today.

That's the privilege of every Christian, and it's not just a matter of studying a book. It's a matter of meeting with a living Person and touching an unseen hand. Even now, I'm writing these words in an empty hotel room in Sioux City, Iowa, and I've been fighting off some nagging worries. But this isn't an empty hotel room. It's as full of the Lord's presence as the Holy of Holies. When I remind myself of that, reality enters the picture.

When I forget God's presence, I'm living in a state of denial, pretense, and error. When I practice His presence, I'm dealing with reality, and reality fosters peace.

I read in the newspaper what happened to Blossie Anderson, a spunky eighty-five-year-old great-grandmother who decided to go fishing along the Saluda River near Greenville, South Carolina. When her sixty-two-year-old son, Louis, tried to dissuade her, she said, "I had you; you didn't have me."

Trudging into the snake-infested swamp with her fishing pole, she fell, struggled back to her feet, became disoriented, and waded through the area in the wrong direction. She finally sat down exhausted, hoping someone would come for her. "I wasn't afraid," she said, "I knew the Lord was with me, and I knew the Lord would bring help, so I just waited."

She waited all day long, and then she spent the night in the wild. The sun rose, and another day came and went. Meanwhile, rescuers mounted an extensive search, but they were looking on the wrong side of the river. The elderly woman just sat where she was, waiting and reminding herself that God was near her.

Rescue workers dragged the river for her body and kept searching. Four days later a rescuer thrashing around the area heard an elderly voice calling, "Hey, mister." The rescuer said, "Granny! How are you?"

"Lord have mercy," she replied, "I've been here for four days without anything to eat." She was taken to Greenville General Hospital where she was treated for exhaustion and dehydration and released. She later told reporters, "I slept at night and rested during the day. I wasn't cold, and I wasn't afraid of them snakes. God was with me, keeping me warm and keeping the snakes' jaws shut."[2]

God's very real presence sustained her. Now, don't ask me why He waited four days before having her rescued. The important thing is He was with her. And don't ask me why you and I are sometimes swamped, stranded, and surrounded by snakes of one sort or another, sometimes for longer than we want. Every believer from biblical times until today has experienced disorienting days—but never a day when the Lord wasn't with us, keeping us warm and keeping the snakes' jaws shut.

Several categories of verses teach us this truth.

The *Nearness* Verses

- Psalm 73:28 says, "But as for me, it is good to be *near* God."
- Psalm 145:18 says, "The LORD is *near* to all who call on him, to all who call on him in truth."
- Moses told the Israelites in Deuteronomy 4:7, "What other nation is so great as to have their gods *near* them the way the LORD our God is near us whenever we pray to him?"

- The psalmist, when beset by foes, said, "Yet you are *near*, LORD, and all your commands are true" (Psalm 119:151).
- Jeremiah said, "You came *near* when I called you, and you said, 'Do not fear'" (Lamentations 3:57).
- Ephesians 2:13 says, "But now in Christ Jesus you who once were far away have been brought *near* by the blood of Christ."
- Hebrews 10:22 says, "Let us draw *near* to God with a sincere heart and with the full assurance that faith brings, having our hearts sprinkled to cleanse us from a guilty conscience."
- James added, "Draw near to God and He will draw *near* to you" (James 4:8 NKJV).
- And this is the word Paul choose to use in Philippians 4:5: "The Lord is *near*."

The *Presence* Verses

- Exodus 33:14 says, "My *Presence* will go with you, and I will give you rest."
- Psalm 46:1 says, "God is our refuge and strength, an ever-*present* help in trouble."
- Psalm 140:13: "Surely the righteous will praise your name, and the upright will live in your *presence*."
- Psalm 16:11 says, "You make known to me the path of life; you will fill me with joy in your *presence*, with eternal pleasures at your right hand."
- Psalm 89:15 speaks of the blessings enjoyed by those who walk in the light of God's *presence*.
- Acts 3:19 promises times of refreshment in the *presence* of the Lord. And when Paul exhorted Timothy in his ministry, he did it "in the *presence* of God and of Christ Jesus" (2 Timothy 4:1).

The *With* Verses

- When the patriarch Joseph was imprisoned in Egypt, the recurring theme was: "But the LORD was *with* him" (Genesis 39:2, 3, 21, 23).

- Isaiah 41:10 says, "So do not fear, for I am *with* you."
- Genesis 28:15 says, "I am *with* you and will watch over you wherever you go."
- Isaiah 57:15 says, "For this is what the high and exalted One says—he who lives forever, whose name is holy: 'I live in a high and holy place, but also *with* the one who is contrite and lowly in spirit.'"
- Psalm 23:4 says, "Even though I walk through the darkest valley, I will fear no evil, for you are *with* me."
- In a similar fashion, Deuteronomy 31:6 says, "Be strong and courageous. Do not be afraid or terrified because of them, for the LORD your God goes *with* you; he will never leave you nor forsake you."
- The gospel of Matthew begins by giving us a special name for our Lord Jesus—Immanuel, which means "God *with* us" (Matthew 1:23); and Matthew ended his gospel with these final words of Jesus: "And surely I am *with* you always, to the very end of the age" (Matthew 28:20).

The *Close* Verses

- Psalm 34:18 says, "The LORD is *close* to the brokenhearted and saves those who are crushed in spirit."
- Proverbs 18:24 says, "There is a friend who sticks *closer* than a brother."
- Isaiah 40:11 says, "He tends his flock like a shepherd: He gathers the lambs in his arms and carries them *close* to his heart."

The psalmist put this in personal terms when he prayed:

> Where can I go from your Spirit?
>> Where can I flee from your presence?
> If I go up to the heavens, you are there;
>> if I make my bed in the depths, you are there.
> If I rise on the wings of the dawn,
>> if I settle on the far side of the sea,
> even there your hand will guide me,
>> your right hand will hold me fast. (Psalm 139:7–10)

Hebrews 13:5–6 says, "'Never will I leave you; never will I forsake you.' So we say with confidence, 'The Lord is my helper; I will not be afraid.'"

In a sense, learning to actualize God's presence is the very definition of revival. Perhaps like you, I'm longing for a new great tsunami of revival to flood our land, and in my studies of the great revivals of the past, the most significant aspect is an intense and unusual awareness of an almost supernatural sense of God's proximity.

Mrs. Hester Rendall told me of working with Rev. Duncan Campbell in the 1950s on the Hebrides Island of Lewis. There had been an intense revival there between 1949 and 1952. Though Hester didn't arrive until 1958, the afterglow of the revival was still evident. One evening she went to a church service and a sense of the presence of the Lord came down so strongly that the people prayed earnestly and hardly dared lift their heads. After a while, Hester's friend leaned over to her and suggested they go home. Hester said, "Why? We've only been here a few minutes."

The friend said, "It's three o'clock in the morning."

Those who study revivals come across story after story like that, in which the intensity of the presence of God comes into a geographical zone so strongly that people can almost feel it, are awed by it, and are brought to instant conviction, conversion, and confidence. More than a hundred years ago, Frank Bartleman described a revival meeting he attended like this: "God came so wonderfully near us the very atmosphere of heaven seemed to surround us. Such a divine 'weight of glory' was upon us, we could only lie on our faces. . . . The Lord seemed almost visible, He was so real."[3]

During the days of evangelist Charles Finney, a revival broke out in Rome, New York, and, according to historian Wesley Duewel,

everyone who came into the village felt an overwhelming sense of God's presence. The sheriff of Utica, some twenty miles away, came on business. He had laughed and mocked at the reports of the revival. As his sleigh crossed the canal one mile outside Rome, an awesome feeling of the presence of God gripped him. The nearer to the village he came, the more powerfully he sensed God's presence. The sheriff found the people in the business establishments so overcome with awe for God they could hardly speak. To try to keep from weeping, the sheriff got up several times and went to the window. He hurried to complete his business and hastened back to Utica. Soon he was converted.[4]

During the Great Awakening of 1857–1858, according to Duewel, the canopy of the presence of the Holy Spirit "seemed to hang like an invisible cloud over many parts of the United States, especially over the eastern seaboard. At times this cloud of God's presence even seemed to extend out to sea. Those on ships approaching the east coast at times felt a solemn, holy influence, even one hundred miles away. . . . Revival began aboard one ship before it reached the coast. People on board began to feel the presence of God and a sense of their own sinfulness. The Holy Spirit convicted them, and they began to pray."[5]

In some revivals, people sensed the presence of God so powerfully they "felt as if the Lord had breathed upon them." And according to one eyewitness during the 1906 Welsh revival, "a sense of the Lord's presence was everywhere. It pervaded, nay, it created the spiritual atmosphere. It mattered not where one went, the consciousness of the reality and nearness of God followed . . . in the homes, on the streets, in the mines and factories, in the schools." Observers described how "the cloud of God's presence hung low over much of Wales for months."[6]

I've never had an experience quite as dramatic as those, but I am learning to recognize God's abiding presence by faith. As wonderful as these revival accounts are, they were momentary reminders of an enduring truth—the Lord is within us, around us, shielding, hovering over, accompanying, abiding with, and attending to us at all times, whether we can physically sense His presence or not. We walk by faith, not by feelings, but that doesn't diminish the reality of His nearness. He has so often reassured us of His presence; how could we doubt Him?

It helps to visualize His nearness. When you awaken in the morning, He is there. When you shower and dress to stagger on to work or school, He is there. When you board the plane, He is there. When the phone rings, He is there. When you get a bad report, He is there. When you face a difficult person, He is there. As you press through the day, working or resting, He is there. As you turn the doorknob and reenter your house at night, He is there. As you retire and go to bed, He is there.

Dr. A. W. Tozer explained, "The practice of the presence of God consists not of projecting an imaginary object from within [our] own mind and then seeking to realize its presence; it is rather to recognize the real presence of the One whom all sound theology declares to be already there."[7]

The chief purpose of prayer is to recognize the presence of the Lord. Someone once asked evangelist Dwight L. Moody how he managed to remain so intimate in his relationship with Christ. He replied:

> I have come to Him as the best friend I have ever found, and I can trust Him in that relationship. I have believed He is Savior; I have believed He is God; I have believed His atonement on the cross is mine, and I have come to Him and submitted myself on my knees, surrendered everything to Him, and got up and stood by His side as my friend, and there isn't any problem in my life, there isn't any uncertainty in my work but I turn and speak to Him as naturally as to someone in the same room, and I have done it these years because I can trust Jesus.[8]

Whatever your burdens today, remember the practice of joy, the practice of gentleness, the practice of nearness, both in terms of His imminent coming and His immediate presence. Those are the starting points in the Bible's strategy for ridding yourself of chronic worry.

Try to learn these simple principles by heart:

Rejoice in the Lord always. I will say it again: Rejoice!
Let your gentleness be evident to all.
The Lord is near.
Do not be anxious about anything.

DISCUSSION QUESTIONS

1. In light of Romans 8:18 and 2 Corinthians 4:17, how should we evaluate our burdens and worries? What current burden can you view differently by doing so against the backdrop of your ultimate future?

2. Read James 4:8 and note its instruction. Now turn to Deuteronomy 4:7 and notice how the latter verse gives us a way to fulfill the former one. How is this reflected in Philippians 4:5–6?

3. What small habit can you begin, tweak, strengthen, or resume this week that will help you better practice the presence of God?

CHAPTER FOUR

THE PRACTICE OF PRAYER

Do not be anxious about anything, but in every situation,
by prayer and petition . . . present your requests to God.

—PHILIPPIANS 4:6

As President William McKinley lay dying from an assassin's bullet in Buffalo, New York, in 1901, the Lord's Prayer was on his lips. Prayer had been a lifelong practice that guided McKinley through his political career and into the presidency. McKinley had been born into a devout Methodist home fifty-eight years before, and born again at age fourteen in a Methodist camp meeting. According to his pastor, A. D. Morton, young McKinley stood up during a youth meeting and said, "I have sinned; I want to be a Christian . . . I give myself to the Savior who has done so much for me."[1]

McKinley's mother, a woman of intense devotion and prayer, taught him to pray by example and encouragement, but his greatest lessons in prayer were forged under the pressures of his duties as President of the United States.

One of his heaviest decisions arose in 1898 regarding the status of the Philippines after the Spanish-American War. One day, a delegation of Methodist leaders came to the White House, and McKinley told them how he had decided to resolve the crisis in the Philippines.

"The truth is, I didn't want the Philippines," he said. "I did not know what to do. . . . I sought counsel from all sides—Democrats as well as Republicans—but got little help. . . . I walked the floor of the White House night after night until midnight, and I am not ashamed to tell you, gentlemen, that I went down on my knees and prayed Almighty God for light and guidance more than one night. And one night late it came to me this way."

McKinley relayed the strategy that developed in his mind as he prayed: that the Philippines should be taken seriously and helped, that the United States should "by God's grace do the very best we could by them as our fellow-men for whom Christ died." McKinley added, "And then I went to bed, and went to sleep and slept soundly."[2]

I love that little slice of presidential history because it illustrates what we should do when we don't know what to do, when our problems seem unsolvable, and when our burdens keep us awake at night. Human advice may help, but nothing compares to taking our burdens to the Lord and processing them through prayer, so as to arrive at guidance, wisdom, and peace.

Prayer is the buffer zone of the soul, where fear is repulsed and where grace and guidance are gained. This is the process described in Philippians 4:6: "Do not be anxious about anything, but in every situation, by prayer and petition, with thanksgiving, present your requests to God."

Perhaps Paul had drawn his principle from Psalm 37: "Do not fret. . . . Trust in the LORD. . . . Take delight in the LORD. . . . Commit your way to the LORD. . . . Be still before the LORD and wait patiently for him; do not fret . . . do not fret—it only leads to evil" (vv. 1–8).

Perhaps he was thinking of Christ's words in Matthew 6: "Pray to your Father, who is unseen . . . pray: 'Our Father in heaven.' . . . Therefore I tell you, do not worry . . . why do you worry? . . . So do not worry. . . . Therefore do not worry" (vv. 6, 9, 25, 28, 31, 34).

Somehow the apostle Paul squeezed, condensed, and compressed two great chapters of the Bible—Psalm 37 and Matthew 6—into one incredible verse—Philippians 4:6—and every phrase of this verse is a wonder of psychology and spirituality.

"DO NOT BE ANXIOUS ABOUT ANYTHING"

The verse begins with a command: "Do not be anxious about anything." The apostle Paul originally wrote these words in the Greek language, and the word he used for anxious was *merimnao*, which comes from a word meaning "to pull in different directions." Worry pulls your mind apart, like a man being drawn and quartered. It rips and ruptures your thoughts and feelings. It makes you feel as though you're being torn in two.

What should do that to us? Nothing! Absolutely nothing!

The older translations of the Bible say emphatically: "In nothing be anxious." In a book of remarkable statements, this one is near the top. *Nothing* should agitate us, because *nothing* can separate us from the love of a God for whom *nothing* is impossible.

The better we grasp the boundless sovereignty of God, the less we'll worry about the everyday burdens of life. If we anchor our hearts in the bottomless depths of Christ's love, nothing can capsize us. When we truly claim the inexhaustible wealth of the Spirit's deposit, we'll be rich in the peace that transcends understanding.

Eugene Peterson's freewheeling translation, *The Message*, states Philippians 4:6–7 like this: "Don't fret or worry. Instead of worrying, pray. Let petitions and praises shape your worries into prayers, letting God know your concerns. Before you know it, a sense of God's wholeness, everything coming together for good, will come and settle you down. It's wonderful what happens when Christ displaces worry at the center of your life."

If this advice were given only here in the Bible, it would still be wonderful and welcomed, but it is *not* given only here. This particular Greek word, *merimnao*, appears several times in the Bible, and these occurrences are consistent in their teaching and represent a divine inoculation against the pandemic of worry.

- *Merimnao* is found in the Greek version of the Old Testament (the Septuagint) in Psalm 55:22, where it is translated "care": "Cast your *cares* on the LORD and he will sustain you; he will never let the righteous be shaken." The writer admits we have "cares," we have situations that tear at our minds, but he tells us what to do with them. Cast them upon the Lord, hand them over to Him, transfer them into His hands, and let Him handle the issues that perplex us.

- We next encounter this word *merimnao* in the Sermon on the Mount in Matthew 6:25–34, where it's translated "worry." Jesus used this term repeatedly in this paragraph, saying, "Therefore I tell you, do not *worry* about your life . . . And why do you *worry* . . . So do not *worry* . . . Therefore do not *worry* about tomorrow." This passage contains our Lord's primary teaching on waging war against worry.

- Jesus used the word *merimnao* again in Matthew 10:19, telling those being persecuted, "But when they arrest you, do not *worry* about what to say or how to say it. At that time you will be given what to say."

- In Luke 10:41, the Lord used this word while gently upbraiding Martha, who had worked herself into an irritable frenzy. He said, "Martha, Martha . . . you are *worried* and upset about many things."

- In 1 Corinthians 7:32, Paul told the Christians to whom he was writing: "I would like you to be free from *concern*"—that is, from anxious concern, from *merimnao*.

- Peter used *merimnao* when he said, "Cast all your *anxiety* on him because he cares for you" (1 Peter 5:7). Notice the "all" in this verse. Nothing is too small for our Lord's concern or too large for His capacity. We should be anxious for nothing, for we can cast all our anxieties on Him.

- And here in Philippians 4:6, the Amplified Bible renders this verse: "Do not be *anxious* or *worried* about anything, but in everything [every circumstance and situation] by prayer and petition with thanksgiving, continue to make your [specific] requests known to God."

How is it possible to obey a command as counterintuitive as Philippians 4:6? Fretting comes as naturally to us as breathing. Some of our earliest memories are the anxieties we encountered in childhood, and we seem to never outgrow our capacity to worry. I should know; I'm an expert on the subject.

Truthfully, I've a hard time accepting the premise of this passage. Anxiety is so deeply ingrained into my personality that I feel guilty when I *don't* worry. When something is deeply troubling me, I feel responsible to worry about it. There's a moral obligation, so it seems, to worry about those things that should logically worry me. How can I shrug off issues that so deeply affect those I love and me? If I don't worry, who will?

Well, that's the point.

As we turn our worries over to the Lord, He goes to work on them. He is able to guard what we have entrusted to Him (2 Timothy 1:12). God, being God, doesn't worry, but He does work. The psalmist said, "It is time for you to act, Lord" (Psalm 119:126). And God can do far more by His action than we can do by our anxiety. According to Ephesians 1:11, God has plans and purposes that work out everything in conformity with the purpose of His will. According to Romans 8:28, all things work out for our good. Sometimes we find ourselves shipwrecked on Omnipotence and stranded on Sovereignty.[3]

We're much better off when Jehovah-Shalom bears the lion's share of our burdens. But what exactly is the process by which we transfer our cares to God and tap into His peace for ourselves? There is only one way to do that—through prayer. Earnest, heartfelt, biblical prayer is the method by which we transfer our legitimate worries into the Lord's mighty hands, and by which He transfers His inexpressible peace into our fragile hearts.

Prayer is the closet where we change clothes and replace a spirit of despair with a garment of praise. It's the bank where we present the promissory notes of God's promises and withdraw endless deposits of grace. It's the darkroom of the soul where negatives become positives. It's the transfer station where the pulse of fear is exchanged for the impulse of faith. It's a currency exchange where we trade in our liabilities for God's abundant life. This is biblical replacement therapy, and it's the duty of the child of God to learn how to displace worrisome thoughts with restorative strength through prevailing prayer, and to do it in every situation.

This verse doesn't describe a natural state, but a supernatural process. According to commentaries I've consulted, the construction of this sentence in the original language as Paul wrote it contains the implication that the Philippians were indeed anxious. They were worried; they'd been upset by threats, dangers, and increasing persecution. They felt the strain of Paul's imprisonment and were apprehensive about the very survival of Christianity in the Roman world. Their anxiety had grown to fever pitch, which was understandable. But Paul told them, as Philippians 4:6 could literally be translated, "Stop worrying and start praying."[4]

Here were Christians in one of the strongest churches in the New Testament, the church in Philippi. They had already braved fires of persecution, and they were dogged in their devotion. Of all Paul's churches, the Philippians were the most generous to him, sending him funds and helping him at every opportunity. A deep bond linked the apostle with the Philippians. Yet some of these believers were torn apart by various alarms. They needed to cease worrying so they could enjoy the transcendent power of God's peace, which would improve their situation all the way around.

This required serious commitment to prayer, to praying systematically, to praying methodically, to praying in faith, to praying in detail. The life of faith is a growing experience, and prayer is an ongoing process of abiding in our Father's presence, meeting with Him at every turn, consulting Him in every plight, and trusting Him with every trial. In prayer, we transfer our problems to the Lord, and He transfers His peace to us. That allows us to rid ourselves of the false guilt we sometimes feel when we stop worrying.

If we live long enough, perhaps we'll reach a level of maturity beyond all worrisome fear. I haven't reached that stage yet, and neither had the Philippians. The Lord was telling us in Philippians 4, in effect: "When you find yourself ripped apart by worry, learn to use the power of My presence through prayer to unleash divine processes that can conquer worry, demolish strongholds, effect change, and inject powerful doses of transcendent peace into your hearts, in every single situation in life."

Sometimes we don't want to stop worrying because it seems wrong to feel lighthearted. We don't want to react flippantly or inappropriately to life's heartaches. But in every situation, our supernatural Lord wants to lighten our hearts and lift the clouds of uneasiness. Things are never as bad as they seem where He is concerned. All His resources are available through prayer, and none of His promises have expired. So stop worrying and start praying, taking time to especially note those items for which you can be thankful.

Our refusal to worry doesn't mean we aren't concerned, nor does it make us passive to circumstances. Concern is appropriate, and wise responses are needed, but worry is unhelpful. The zone between concern and worry is a slippery slope. I've often wondered how to know, at any given time, if I'm reasonably concerned or unreasonably alarmed. It's a difficult median, but here's the key: When our concern is healthy in nature, it doesn't debilitate us. When it begins to feel debilitating, it has morphed into worry, which becomes a vicious cycle. I don't know about you, but sometimes I worry myself sick over how worried I am that I'm worried.

When worry barges into our brains, it brings along a gang of accomplices—discouragement, fear, exhaustion, despair, anguish, hopeless- ness, pain, obsession, distraction, foreboding, irritation, impatience—none of which are friends of the Holy Spirit. We have to throw the bums out of our hearts and minds. Prayer is how we open the door, shove them out, and let the peace of God rush in to secure our thoughts and feelings.

"BUT IN EVERY SITUATION"

How often should that happen? It should happen "in every situation." Every single one! That phrase "in every situation" is indicative of the book of Philippians, where various forms of this idea crop up everywhere. Paul was writing from jail, where he had faced a host of discomforting circumstances. He talked about what had happened to him, what might happen to him, and about the circumstances and situations that had come unwelcomed into his life.

- In Philippians 1:12, he said, "I want you to know, brothers and sisters, that what has happened to me . . ."
- In verse 19, he again talked about "what has happened to me."

- In verse 27, he told them, "Whatever happens, conduct yourselves in a manner worthy of the gospel."
- In Philippians 2:23, he said he would send Timothy to them, "as soon as I see how things go."
- In Philippians 4:6, he used the phrase "in every situation."
- In verse 11, he spoke his ability to remain composed, "whatever the circumstances."
- In verse 12, he said, "I have learned the secret of being content in any and every situation."

All these phrases indicate things were happening to Paul outside his control. But rather than worrying about them, he had learned he could bring them to the Lord and pray about every one of them, knowing that under God's providential control each situation would, in the final analysis, turn in a good-ward and in a God-ward direction. The Lord's providential ordering of all things for the good of His children is just as certain as the resurrection of Christ from the grave on the third day.

Sometimes we learn this on the fly. Not long ago a New Zealand pilot named Owen B. Wilson wanted to do something special for his friend, Grant Stubbs, who was celebrating a birthday. Wilson offered to take his friend flying in a two-seat, micro-light plane. The two men took off after church on Sunday from the South Island town of Blenheim in the Marlborough region, flying northeast over the Golden Bay, around hills and over gorgeous landscapes and seascapes along the northern tip of the island. The weather was crystal clear and a panorama of splendor spread before them. But as they crossed a tall mountain, the engine sputtered and died. The plane began losing altitude, and at that point Wilson could see nothing but steep mountainsides descending into a treacherous sea.

Both men were Christians and they prayed instantly and earnestly. Stubbs, who had grown up in a minister's home and been involved in Youth for Christ and Campus Life, prayed aloud as Wilson manhandled the controls. When it appeared the two would fly into a mountain, Stubbs cried: "Lord, please help us to get over that steep ledge!"

They skimmed over the ridge, and Grant began praying, "Lord, we need to find somewhere to land!" Just when all hope seemed gone, the men saw a small strip of land almost hidden between two ridges. Wilson steered the plane in that direction. They glided into the narrow valley and touched down, bouncing to a stop. They both shouted, "Thank You, Lord!"

They looked up and just in front of them was a huge twenty-foot sign that said, "Jesus is Lord!"

As it turned out, the field belonged to a Christian retreat center, which explained the billboard. The owners, who ran out to greet their unexpected guests, told them the field was usually full of livestock, but on this day all the animals were standing along the edge of the field, as though giving them room to land.[5]

Many times we fly into anxious situations in life. Our engines stall. We encounter turbulence. Perhaps we're bracing for a crash and things seem hopeless. But in every situation we practice the power of prayer, and that's how we discover the incredible truth that Jesus is Lord.

"BY PRAYER AND PETITION . . . PRESENT YOUR REQUESTS TO GOD"

Continuing Philippians 4:6, Paul described more precisely how we address God about our issues. He used the words *prayer* and *petition*, and the phrase "present your requests." *Prayer* is a general word for all our communication with God. *Petition* is a more specific term, referring to asking God for help regarding certain needs. It's one thing to chat with a friend; it's another to ask him for a favor. When we need multiple favors, we become even more specific and *present our requests*. While these phrases are very similar, the triple use of them indicates the intensity we need in putting this opportunity into practice. We should pray, pray some more, and keep on praying. As Dr. J. Oswald Sanders once said about a certain matter, "There is praying in detail to be done."[6]

None of us does this perfectly, but we can improve, we can learn, and we can grow in prevailing prayer. One of the keys is the diversification of our methods. Prayer can be practiced in countless ways. It's not just a matter of bowing our heads, folding our hands, and closing our eyes. In fact, when I went through the Bible studying the physical postures employed by biblical characters when they prayed, I was astounded to find no example—not a single one—of anyone in the Bible who actually did close their eyes or bow their heads or fold their hands when they prayed. There's nothing wrong with such practices, of course, but the heroes of Scripture more often opened their eyes, lifted their arms, and looked upward when they prayed.

They prayed kneeling, sitting, lying down, falling prostrate, standing up, walking, under the canopy of the sky, in their rooms, in their closets, on the rooftops, in the caves, and in the belly of the whale. They prayed silently and aloud. They prayed privately and corporately. They prayed with sighs, with spoken words, with shouts, and with songs. They prayed long prayers and short ones. They wrote out their prayers. They prayed with tears and with laughter. They prayed coming and going, at home and abroad, day and night. They offered prayers of confession, thanksgiving, praise, power, supplication, and petition. They prayed in desperation and in delight. In the Psalms, they often began their prayers in despair and ended them in praise, never the other way around.

The Bible acknowledges the diversity of prayer methods when we're told, "And pray in the Spirit on all occasions with all kinds of prayers and requests. With this in mind, be alert and always keep on praying" (Ephesians 6:18).

When I'm in the midst of an anxious episode, I often find myself at a desk with my journal and an open Bible, asking God to stabilize not just the situation but me as well. I write out my fears and emotions, because stating them makes them more manageable. Then I search the Scripture to find verses that comfort my heart, and I write those down too. Then I pray aloud, sometimes writing out my prayers, sometimes pacing the room, kneeling, falling on my face, or going for a prayer walk, as I plead for God's help. Other times I'll seek out someone to pray with—my wife, my prayer partner, or a close friend.

Sometimes our prayers are extended. Daniel and Nehemiah fasted and prayed for many weeks over certain matters. On the other hand, the publican in Luke 18:13 simply beat his fist against his chest and said seven words, "God, have mercy on me, a sinner."

Occasionally I'll find a phrase from Scripture to think about repetitively whenever fear or panic rises. A good example is Matthew 6:10, which says, "Your will be done, on earth as it is in heaven." That's an all-purpose plea from the lips of Jesus that helps me know what to pray when other words fail: "Lord, Your will be done in this situation, as it's done in heaven." Whenever the tide of worry rises in my heart, I pause and deliberately pray, "Lord, may Your will be done right now in this thing." We can sense the poignancy of this phrase because at the end of His earthly life, our Lord circled back to it, saying, in the Garden of Gethsemane, "May your will be done" (Matthew 26:42).

Finding phrases in the Bible is a powerful method of prayer. An acquaintance of mine who faced a terminal illness said he became too weak to pray very long at once, but phrases of Scripture would come to his mind, and he turned those into prayers that he offered throughout the day. From his years of Bible study and Scripture memory, he had an endless supply of materials to fuel the lamplight of his flickering prayers in the evening of life.

When we use the words of Scripture in prayer, we're praying as God would have us pray. The Bible is an immense prayer book, filled with verses that can be turned into prayers as easily as substituting someone's name for the original wording. For example, if you're worried about a struggling child or family member, consider Colossians 4:12: "Epaphras, who is one of you and a servant of Christ Jesus, sends greetings. He is always wrestling in prayer for you, that you may stand firm in all the will of God, mature and fully assured."

We can always adapt this verse into a prayer for our loved ones: "Lord, I am wrestling in prayer for them, that they may stand firm in all Your will, mature and fully assured."

Having found a prayer that meets your need, it's important to offer it with the element of faith. We may not always have a great faith, but we can always have faith in a great God and in His unfailing promises. The Lord expects our trust, and it's insulting when we doubt the very words Christ died to confirm.

Prayer shouldn't be a hamster wheel of worry; it should be a launchpad of faith. We take our burdens to the Lord and leave them there. The book of James tells us to pray whenever we're in trouble, for the prayer of faith can make the difference. "The prayer of a righteous person is powerful and effective" (5:16).

There is, then, diversity in our prayer methods, but I've found it helpful to think of prayer in three distinct forms.

Everyday Prayer

The most vital for me is everyday prayer. We must pray regularly, systematically, methodically, and daily. The prophet Daniel was so habitual in prayer that even his enemies knew his habits. Daniel knelt and prayed in the morning before going into his daily work; he came home and prayed during his midday break; and he prayed in the evening before going to bed (Daniel 6:10).

When I was nineteen, I had mentors who impressed on me the importance of beginning my day with morning devotions, and this habit has kept me afloat for forty-six years. I discuss my own procedures in my book *Mastering Life Before It's Too Late*, but here's the short form: After arising and showering in the morning, I sit down at a small upstairs desk where I briefly jot down a few lines in my journal, read God's Word, work on some verse or another that I'm memorizing, and open up my prayer lists, thanking God for His blessings and asking for His intervention in things concerning me. I often pray aloud. Before leaving the spot, I consult my calendar and jot out a proposed agenda for the day. Psalm 143:8 says, "Let the morning bring me word of your unfailing love, for I have put my trust in you. Show me the way I should go, for to you I entrust my life."

It's as simple as that, but nothing goes right about my day if I neglect the practice.

Perhaps the morning hour doesn't fit your schedule. It's not a matter of having a time of *morning* prayer but of *daily* prayer, whenever works best. The things that mean most to us are the things we do daily. That's the glue of life that holds everything together. Jesus told us to go into our inner rooms and shut the door and talk to our heavenly Father in secret (Matthew 6:6). This implies a definite time and place for meeting privately with God in a way that allows us to realize and recognize His presence, which, after all, is the intent of Philippians 4:5–6: "The Lord is near . . . in every situation, by prayer and petition . . . present your requests to God."

Some people keep a prayer list on the flyleaf of their Bibles. Others simply keep a mental list. My friend Don Wyrtzen told me how, over the years, he's developed a mental template that guides his prayers, based on his reading of the book of Ephesians. He begins his prayer time with an emphasis on the spiritual aspects of his life—praising God for who He is, what He does, knowing Him, loving Him, and trusting Him. Don then moves to the relational aspects of his life, praying for himself, his wife, his children and grandchildren, his siblings, his extended family and friends, and those who need the Lord. Finally he prays about the vocational aspects of his life, his calling and work, his finances and opportunities. He doesn't use a written list, but this mental outline goes with him wherever he travels and structures his regular daily prayer sessions with God. When he prays for friends across the country, Don told me, he often moves from east to west, starting in Maine and praying for friends across America, ending in Southern California.[7]

Perhaps Paul did something similar. It must have been hard for him to keep written lists due to his unpredictable conditions. But prayer is extraordinarily adaptive to all situations so long as we practice it every day.

If this is a new habit for you, please persevere with it. When I mentor young adults in their prayer habits, I ask them to make unbreakable commitments for a period of time, with accountability measures in place. Learning to pray takes determination, but it's worth it. It can save you from a fretful life.

D-Day Prayer

Sometimes we need to practice D-Day prayer in times of unusual crisis or fear. Multitudes thronged Washington's Union Station on the morning of

June 6, 1944, coming and going, crisscrossing the great hall, headed to their respective trains. For weeks, there had been rumors of an impending D-Day, when Allied Forces would invade Europe to turn the tide of World War II. On this morning, something incredible happened. No announcement was made from the loudspeakers, and there were no radios or newsboys shouting the message. But suddenly everyone just stopped. Conversations ceased. The invasion had begun, and news passed in whispers that American boys were storming the beaches in Normandy.

A beam of sunlight pierced the room like a cathedral. Suddenly a woman dropped to her knees and folded her hands. Near her a man knelt down. Then another, then another, until all throughout the station, people knelt in silent prayer beside the hard wooden benches. A great railroad station in our nation's capital had become a palace of prayer.

Then slowly the woman rose to her feet. The man beside her rose, too, and within seconds Union Station was alive with motion and sound again. All across America, people paused to pray. The New York Stock Exchange opened the day with a time for prayer. The *New York Daily News* ran the Lord's Prayer on its front page. Prayer rallies gathered across the United States.[8]

That night, President Franklin Roosevelt went on the radio to address the nation, and he gave arguably the most moving speech in American history. I've seen the original draft in FDR's Presidential Library, and I still get choked up when I read it or hear a recording of the broadcast:

> My fellow Americans, last night, when I spoke with you about the fall of Rome, I knew at that moment that troops of the United States and our Allies were crossing the Channel in another and greater operation. It has come to pass with success thus far. And so, in this poignant hour, I ask you to join with me in prayer: Almighty God, Our sons, pride of our nation, this day have set upon a mighty endeavor, a struggle to preserve our Republic, our religion, and our civilization, and to set free a suffering humanity. Lead them straight and true; give strength to their arms, stoutness to their hearts, steadfastness in their faith. They will need Thy blessings.[9]

After praying for the men in the armed forces, Roosevelt went on to pray for those back home—fathers, mothers, children, wives, sisters, and brothers. He ended his prayer with the words of the Lord Jesus: *Thy will be done, almighty God. Amen.* FDR's entire speech was nothing but prayer, but nothing was more needed at that moment in our nation's history.

From time to time, each of us faces our own individual D-Days, when we encounter difficult decisions, distresses, disasters, disappointments, or discouragements. Burdens press against us, foes oppress us, storms batter us. But no burden, foe, or storm can threaten the throne of God, which is why we come boldly to the throne of grace where we obtain mercy and find grace to help in time of need (Hebrews 4:16).

On every occasion. In every situation. Wherever we are—a train station, an airplane seat, a hospital bed, a courtroom, a cell, the cab of your truck, or the closet of your bedroom—wherever we are can become a cathedral of prayer and praise.

In the book of 1 Samuel, a woman named Hannah had terrible family problems. She went to the tabernacle at Shiloh, and "in her deep anguish Hannah prayed to the Lord, weeping bitterly. . . . Hannah was praying in her heart, and her lips were moving but her voice was not heard. . . . [She said,] 'I was pouring out my soul to the Lord' (1:10, 13, 15). After Hannah gave her burden to the Lord, "she went her way and ate something, and her face was no longer downcast" (v. 18).

God had not yet answered her prayer, but she had turned her worry list into a prayer list, cast her burden on the Lord, claimed His victory, and changed her attitude accordingly.

We see this pattern repeatedly in the Bible. Abraham and Sarah prayed in their barrenness; Jacob pleaded for his sons; Moses prayed for water from the rock; Joshua prayed for victory in battle; Gideon prayed while hiding from the Midianites; David prayed while running from the armies of Saul; Hezekiah prayed during the Assyrian invasion; Jeremiah prayed as his culture collapsed around him; Daniel prayed for insights about the last days; Nehemiah prayed while building the walls around Jerusalem; Jesus prayed on the eve of Calvary; the early church prayed for boldness amid persecution; the apostles prayed for power from on high; John prayed when exiled to the island of Patmos.

In times of great crisis, we must pray and trust God with burdens heavier than we can bear. This isn't a happy-go-lucky affair. It's spiritual warfare, for, as Cameron Thompson wrote, "there comes a time, in spite of our soft, modern ways, when we must be desperate in prayer, when we must wrestle, when we must be outspoken, shameless, and importunate . . . plowing through principalities and powers, inviting His almighty power into our desperate needs."[10]

Despite the intensity of these special times of prayer, the process is remarkably simple. African American hymnist Charles A. Tindley once counseled a man who was a chronic worrier. After listening to him awhile, Tindley advised him to take his burdens to the Lord and leave them there; as Tindley later pondered the advice he gave, he turned it into a beloved gospel song.

> *If the world from you withhold of its silver and its gold,*
> *And you have to get along on meager fare,*
> *Just remember, in His Word, how He feeds the little bird;*
> *Take your burden to the Lord and leave it there.*[11]

Through-the-Day Prayers

There's one other kind of prayer that helps us in every situation— through-the-day prayers. Prayer isn't just something we do during regular devotions or at moments of crisis. The Bible tells us to pray without ceasing. Prayer is a constantly recurring activity during each day.

In *Lessons from My Parents*, Stephanie Porter recalled a time when she and her brothers were putting on their snow gear to play outside, sledding and building igloos. But their mother stopped them. She had lost her wedding ring and was frantically looking for it. She asked the children to kneel and pray with her. They did so, and as soon as the "Amen," was finished, they jumped up to resume dressing. "My five-year-old bother slipped a foot into his snow boot and immediately pulled it back off," Stephanie wrote. "He turned the boot upside down and out slipped my mom's wedding ring. . . . We momentarily forgot about the snow and ran excitedly to show our mom that our prayer worked."[12]

The memory of that impromptu prayer stayed with Stephanie, and it has transcended generations. Stephanie wrote: "Now that I have my own kids, I teach them about faith. We pray every day before school, meals, and bedtime. . . . I hope my daughters will learn faith from me, as I learned it from my mother."[13]

When the biblical hero Nehemiah heard of the dilapidated condition of Israel's security in the first chapter of his book, he sat down and wept and mourned and prayed for several days, finally composing his words into a written prayer, which is recorded in Nehemiah 1. In the next chapter, King Artaxerxes asked Nehemiah what was wrong and what he needed. Nehemiah 2:4–5 is very instructive: "The king said to me, 'What is it you want?' Then I prayed to the God of heaven, and I answered the king."

I wonder if Artaxerxes noticed the slight pause that proceeded Nehemiah's answer. Before speaking to the earthly king before him, Nehemiah sent up a silent plea to the heavenly King above him—and his request was granted.

I have a friend who keeps a perpetual prayer list on a sheet of paper carefully folded in his pocket. It's always there, which allows him to pray whenever and wherever he is. He can't keep up with a notebook or journal, but he's never without his prayer list. When waiting to board a plane or stopped at a red light, he can glance down at his list and begin praying where he left off, and in this way he prays periodically from daybreak to bedtime.

Even without a list, we can learn to mutter prayers all day long, talking to the Lord as naturally as to a companion who never leaves our side. When prayer and quoting Scripture becomes as natural as saying our names or greeting a friend, we'll be on our way to spiritual maturity and transcendent peace.

I began this chapter with a story about a president who believed in prayer. Let me end it by describing a general who does the same. Charles Krulak, the thirty-first Commandant of the Marine Corps, was involved in Operation Desert Storm in the early 1990s. One of his biggest challenges was providing water for the troops. He was always careful to position his forces in areas with plenty of wells. But on one occasion, thousands of troops were ordered into a barren part of the desert where conditions were bone dry and drilling for wells proved futile.

General Krulak is a Christian who habitually gathered all his willing staff every morning at 7:15 for prayer. On this day, he and his staff were on their knees praying about their need for water when a colonel interrupted Krulak, saying, "Sir, could you come with me? It's important."

When Krulak asked what it was, the colonel said, "I want to show you."

The colonel took Krulak down a road constructed by the Marine Corps and there, rising out of the ground, was a large pipe, about forty yards from the road. A bar on the pipe formed the shape of a cross. At the base were a green diesel generator and a red pump. There was also a tank containing one thousand gallons of diesel fuel and four new batteries still wrapped in plastic. Krulak and the colonel wondered how they could have missed seeing this. Twenty thousand troops had traveled this road, and no one had reported seeing this colorful well.

Krulak went over and looked at the contraption but there was no key to start the generator. He looked at his officer and said, "God did not put this here to be defeated by the lack of a key." He reached over and pushed the start button, and the generator fired up. The pump started, and it began drawing water. There was enough water to supply 100,000 gallons of water each day.

Major General Krulak later told this story in Washington, saying: "There was no way anyone could have driven down that road and not seen that well and equipment painted in multiple colors. That well is the result of prayers of righteous men and women praying in America."[14]

The Greek philosopher Archimedes said, "Give me a lever and a place to stand, and I'll move the world." He was referring to one of the world's simplest machines, the lever, in which a long beam placed against a fulcrum can move large objects using the power of leverage. The practice of prayer is our leverage throughout life, and the prayers of righteous people have long arms. Our prayers can move heaven and earth, for the prayers of righteous people are powerful and effective—daily prayers, D-Day prayers, and through-the-day prayers.

So rejoice in the Lord; let your gentleness be evident; remember the Lord's nearness; and do not be anxious about anything, but in every situation, by prayer and petition, present your requests to God. The world offers no better antidote to worry, for there is none. This is God's prescription for a better life.

DISCUSSION QUESTIONS

1. If you had a cell phone linked to heaven, giving you instant access to God Himself whenever you turned it on, how would you feel? How often would you use it? If you could call and discuss with Him any problem in your life, what would it be?

2. How do Paul's words in Philippians 4:5–6 reflect the teachings of Psalm 37:1–9? Of Matthew 6:5–33? How would you could summarize all three of these passages into a simple statement?

3. When Paul said, "Don't be anxious about anything," was he speaking in hyperbole or exaggerating the command? How literally should we practice this advice? In what area of your life can you put this into practice today?

CHAPTER FIVE

THE PRACTICE OF THANKSGIVING

. . . with thanksgiving . . .

—PHILIPPIANS 4:6

John Brockman is a literary agent and scientific writer who specializes in bringing together the planet's best minds to contribute to his website and online magazine. He's renowned for his access to Nobel Prize winners, brilliant thinkers, and world-class scientists and technologists. Few, if any, of these thinkers are Christians, but they all make interesting contributions to Brockman's journal.

Every year on the anniversary of the launch of his website, Brockman and his editors craft a different question and invite their high-octane participants to answer it. The questions vary from year to year, but they're always remarkably perceptive. Recently the question was very simple: "What Should We Be Worried About?"

If you are predisposed toward anxiety, you may want to skip the next paragraph, because you'll discover whole new issues to upset you. The best minds in the world are frightened about things I'd never before considered. All the contributors wrote small essays on what most worried them, and here are some of the titles:

- Chinese Eugenics
- The Black Hole of Finance
- The Underpopulation Bomb
- The Anthropocebo Effect
- Science Has Not Brought Us Closer to Understanding Cancer
- The Role of Microorganisms in Cancer
- The Exploding Number of New Illegal Drugs
- The Rise of Genomic Instability
- The Nightmare Scenario for Fundamental Physics
- Quantum Mechanics
- The Fragility of Complex Systems

One professor said he's worried because "global cooperation is failing and we don't know why."[1] Another is worried because we're "living in a world of cascading crises."[2] In his essay, John Tooby, an evolutionist and noted professor, said:

> The universe is relentlessly, catastrophically dangerous, on scales that menace not just communities, but civilizations and our species as well. A freakish chain of improbable accidents produced the bubble of conditions that was necessary for the rise of life, our species, and technological civilization. If we continue to drift obliviously inside this bubble, taking its continuation for granted, then inevitably—sooner or later—physical or human-triggered events will push us outside, and we will be snuffed out like a candle in a hurricane.[3]

Another contributor said he was most worried by the "Unknown Unknowns" ahead of us, and yet another eminent professor had a one-word title for his essay—"Armageddon."[4]

Few of us lose sleep over cosmic threats until they're brought home to us in an immediate way. Most of our worries are closer at hand. But whether our concerns are intergalactic or interpersonal, we exist in an anxious world that skips along the edges of danger and difficulty. No one knows what the next hour or day will bring. Yet the Bible directs us to live beyond the pale of worry. We are told emphatically: "Do not worry about anything." We must take every word of Philippians 4:6 as holy counsel to be instantly and thoroughly obeyed: "Do not be anxious about anything, but in every situation, by prayer and petition, with thanksgiving, present your requests to God."

Perhaps you noticed in the last chapter I had little to say about two critical words in that verse: "with thanksgiving." That's because they deserve a chapter of their own. They represent the fifth step in overcoming worry—the practice of gratitude or thanksgiving. In a world where we're frustrated by everything from the fragility of complex systems to the complexity of our entertainment systems, we need to nurture thankful hearts and minds full of gratitude.

Try this experiment. Read Philippians 4:6 (NKJV) aloud, leaving out the words "with thanksgiving." Say the verse like this:

> Be anxious for nothing,
> but in everything by prayer and supplication,
> let your requests be made known to God.

Now try it God's way and emphasize the phrase "with thanksgiving."

> Be anxious for nothing,
> but in everything by prayer and supplication,
> *with thanksgiving,*
> let your requests be made known to God.

The verse sounds reasonable either way, but the addition of "with thanksgiving" adds a dimension that melts away worry like winter's ice on a sunny day. No matter our crisis or concern, there are always notable items for which we can be thankful, and finding them is critical to worrying less and living more.

In any given situation, whether trivial or horrendous, there are always observable items we can discover and acknowledge with thanksgiving. If we don't find those items, focus on them, and thank God for them, we cannot overcome anxiety. Gratitude is to worry what antibiotics are to an infection. The old practice of "counting our blessings" is an effective modern treatment for what's ailing the mind. Giving thanks is essential to mental health.

In her book *It's My Turn*, Billy Graham's wife, Ruth, told of awaking in the early morning, about three o'clock, in another country. She was exhausted, but the name of someone she loved flashed into her mind like an electric shock. She wrote:

> So I lay there and prayed for the one who was trying hard to run away from God. When it is dark and the imagination runs wild, there are fears that only a mother can understand.
>
> Suddenly the Lord said to me, *Quit studying the problems and start studying the promises*. Now God has never spoken to me audibly, but there is no mistaking when He speaks. So I turned on the light, got out my Bible, and the first verse that came to me was Philippians 4:6. "Be anxious for nothing, but in everything by prayer and supplication, *with thanksgiving*, let your requests be made known to God."[5]

Ruth read and pondered that verse as though seeing it for the first time. "Suddenly," she wrote:

> I realized the missing ingredient in my prayers had been "with thanksgiving." So I put down my Bible and spent time worshipping Him for who He is and what He is. This covers more territory than any one mortal can comprehend. Even contemplating what little we do know dissolves doubts, reinforces faith, and restores joy. I began to thank God for giving me this one I loved so dearly in the first place. I even thanked Him for the difficult spots which taught me so much.
>
> And you know what happened? It was as if suddenly someone turned on the lights in my mind and heart, and the little fears and worries which, like mice and cockroaches, had been nibbling away in the darkness, suddenly scuttled for cover.[6]

THE THEOLOGY OF GRATITUDE

I believe that's what the apostle Paul learned as well. As we've already speculated, he seemed, by nature, high-strung and keyed up. But Paul had learned to weave the concept of "with thanksgiving" into the fabric of his thinking, and gratitude appeared incessantly in his writing. He spoke of it in theological terms, as though it were as important as any other doctrine. We could rightly call Paul the apostle of gratitude.

This shows up clearly in the letter that immediately follows Philippians. In our Bible, we come to the letter to the Philippians with its four chapters, then we turn the page to the epistle to the Colossians. It's as if the Holy Spirit wanted to take these two words in Philippians 4:6—"with thanksgiving"—and further expound on them throughout the four chapters of Colossians, where we find Paul's theology of gratitude on every page.

"We always *thank God,*" Paul wrote in Colossians 1:3. Then down in verse 10, Paul commanded the Colossians: "Live a life worthy of the Lord and please him in every way." Here's how do we do that:

> bearing fruit in every good work, growing in the knowledge of God, being strengthened with all power according to his glorious might so that you may have great endurance and patience, and *giving joyful thanks to the Father,* who has qualified you to share in the inheritance of his holy people in the kingdom of light. (vv. 10–12)

Colossians 2 continues the theme: "So then, just as you received Christ Jesus as Lord, continue to live your lives in him, rooted and built up in him, strengthened in the faith as you were taught, and *overflowing with thankfulness*" (vv. 6–7).

Imagine you were a river. If thanksgiving were measured like water, would you be a dry gulch, a trickle, brimming at the banks, or overflowing at flood stage? How you and I answer that simple question says something about our mental health and our ability to manage our anxieties.

The next chapter of Colossians extends the connection between gratitude and peace of mind: "Let the peace of Christ rule in your hearts. . . . And *be thankful*. . . . And whatever you do, whether in word or in deed, do it all in the name of the Lord Jesus, *giving thanks* to God the Father through him" (Colossians 3:15–17).

Then we come to Colossians 4, which commands: "Devote yourselves to prayer, being watchful and *thankful*" (v. 2).

This theme isn't just found in Philippians and Colossians, of course. It runs like a stream from the first pages of Scripture to the last ones, and it's interlaced into the Bible as fully as any doctrine. Dr. Al Mohler wrote: "Thanksgiving is a deeply theological act, rightly understood. As a matter of fact, thankfulness is theology in microcosm—a key to understanding what we really believe about God, ourselves, and the world we experience."[7]

THE PSYCHOLOGY OF GRATITUDE

The great Bible teacher Harry Ironside said, "We would worry less if we praised more. Thanksgiving is the enemy of discontent and dissatisfaction."[8] In simplest terms, that means you can instantly lessen the level of your anxiety by finding something for which to immediately thank God. It works like this for me: If something triggers an anxious episode, I have to pull myself together and ask, "As bad as this seems, it's not as bad as it could be. In fact, here are some things I can thank God for in the middle of this mess." I then use my brainpower to compile a list of blessings.

It's like the seesaw we played on as children. When the poundage at one end counterbalances the other, the law of gravity goes into effect. The weight of our blessings is sometimes heavy enough to flip our worries into the air like a bully caught off guard.

This is classic Christianity, but something interesting has happened in recent times in the secular world. An entire science of gratitude has arisen, as legions of experts are discovering the psychological power of gratitude. Most of these modern scholars aren't coming at thanksgiving and gratitude from a distinctively Christian point of view, but they're nonetheless discovering how a biblical attitude—thanksgiving—has a profound effect on the human spirit.

One of the foremost researchers in this field is Dr. Robert A. Emmons of the University of California, Davis. In his book *Thanks! How Practicing Gratitude Can Make You Happier*, he explained how each of us is born with certain preset elements to our personalities. Just as each of us has a unique and individual body, so each of us has a unique and individual personality. Some are more introverted; some more extroverted. Some are more inclined to be happy; some prone toward melancholy. Some are strong-willed; others are acquiescent. Some are loud; others are quiet. According to Dr. Emmons, "Current psychological dogma states that one's capacity for joy is biologically set."[9]

He wrote: "Each person appears to have a set-point for happiness. . . . Each person has a chronic or characteristic level of happiness. According to this idea, people have happiness set-points to which they inevitably return following disruptive life events."[10]

But Dr. Emmons has done innovative research to demonstrate there is one quality that, if developed and practiced, can actually change our set-point for happiness. We can change the gauges of our personalities in an upward and happier direction if we deliberately and doggedly work on improving our habits of gratitude and thanksgiving.

Emmons wrote:

We discovered scientific proof that when people regularly engage in a systematic cultivation of gratitude, they experience a variety of measurable benefits: psychological, physical, and interpersonal. The evidence on gratitude contradicts the widely held view that all people have a "set-point" of happiness that cannot be reset by any known means: in some cases, people have reported that gratitude led to transformative life changes.[11]

He concluded, "Our groundbreaking research has shown that grateful people experience higher levels of positive emotions such as joy, enthusiasm, love, happiness and optimism, and that the practice of gratitude as a discipline protects a person from the destructive impulses of envy, resentment, greed, and bitterness."[12]

Another book on this subject is *The Gratitude Diaries* by Janice Kaplan, who, as editor-in-chief of *Parade* magazine, led a survey funded by the John Templeton Foundation on the subject of gratitude and its impact. Her research became personal to her, and she was affected by something she read in the *Journal of Social and Clinical Psychology*: "Gratitude may have the highest connection to mental health and happiness of any of the personality traits studied."[13]

Kaplan determined to become her own social scientist. "I wanted to see what happened when I developed an attitude of gratitude," she said. Instead of doing this casually, she determined to make a full commitment to get as much information as she could and report and record her findings. She sought advice at every turn from experts and psychologists, and she consulted books by philosophers and psychologists and theologians.[14]

She took up one of Dr. Emmons's suggested habits and began keeping a gratitude journal. "One of the consistent findings in the research was the value of keeping a gratitude journal," she said. "Researchers have found that people who write down three things they're grateful for every night (or even a few times a week) improve their well-being and lower their risk of depression. The results have been repeated over and over. Keeping a gratitude journal can even dramatically improve your ability to get a good night's sleep."[15]

Kaplan conducted her own one-year experiment, and the subtitle of her book summarizes her findings: *The Gratitude Diaries: How a Year of Looking on the Bright Side Can Transform Your Life.*

THE METHODOLOGY OF GRATITUDE

I'm tempted to feel some fiendish delight when modern researchers spend large sums of money to "discover" something the Bible announced long ago. But as it relates to studying gratitude, secular researchers run into an impassable roadblock when they try to answer the question: "To whom are we thankful?" They may uncover the benefits of feeling thankful, but how can we be thankful to a purely impersonal naturalistic universe?

We can always be thankful to certain people who love or befriend us. But what about all the blessings that can't be credited to friends, loved ones, or ruling authorities? What about the wonders of sky, sea, and land? What about life itself, the privilege of living on a spinning blue marble in a vast universe of fathomless complexity?

The ability to say, "Thank You, Lord," is among the most wonderful things about being a follower of Jesus Christ. We can enter His gates with thanksgiving and His courts with praise. We don't thank and praise God merely to gain the psychological benefits of doing so. We thank and praise Him because He is the God from whom all blessings flow. But this gratitude boomerangs into benefits the world can never know. Emotional benefits. Psychological blessings. Spiritual experiences, which our passage in Philippians 4 labels as transcendent: "With thanksgiving, present your requests to God. And the peace of God, which transcends all understanding, will guard your hearts and minds in Christ Jesus."

And consider this: Jesus-followers are the only people who can truly thank God in a Christly way for all His blessings. What a tragedy if we fail to do it. The Lutheran minister Martin Rinkart wrote a hymn of thanksgiving to rally his village of Ellenburg, Saxony, during the ravages of the Thirty Years' War. Rinkart was the only surviving pastor in town, and he sometimes conducted as many as fifty funerals a day. Yet he kept himself and his village sane by finding items of thanksgiving, even among the carnage. He converted this attitude into one of our great hymns:

> *Now thank we all our God, with heart and hands and voices,*
> *Who wondrous things has done, in whom this world rejoices;*
> *Who from our mothers' arms has blessed us on our way*
> *With countless gifts of love, and still is ours today.*[16]

How can we cultivate a spirit of thanksgiving like that?

My friend Linda Derby once faced a health crisis in her family. Her daughter-in-law, Becky Derby, mother of two little boys, was diagnosed with cancer, and it was a devastating case. On the day the bad news hit, Linda said it felt as if a black cloud of poisonous insects was swarming around her head, and she was panicked with fear.

She later wrote:

> As I sought God and started to pray, He brought to mind the words of the Apostle Paul to the Philippians: "Don't worry about anything; instead, pray about everything. Tell God what you need, and thank him for all he has done. Then you will experience God's peace, which exceeds anything we can understand" (Philippians 4:6–7 NLT).
>
> After this epiphany, I decided to really get serious about talking to God. I started telling Him everything our family was experiencing, our worries, anxiety, fear, depression, anger, and uncertainty—I told God what we wanted, such as peace and assurance that Becky would be all right. Then I tried to think of all the things God had done that I was thankful for—just like Paul had instructed. To my surprise, there were many good things that had recently happened.[17]

She went on to list five distinct blessings, and she was surprised at how she had nearly overlooked them. By the end of the evening, she said, the cloud of insects had been swept away by the Spirit of God and she was able to go to bed with peace in her heart and enjoy a restful night of sleep.[18]

If Linda had omitted that last stop of thanksgiving, a few of those insects would have buzzed through her mind all night. "With thanksgiving" is an indelible part of the verse and an invaluable habit for dispelling the cloud of worry from our minds.

Here are some habits I've gleaned from others and tried for myself in my efforts to develop an accelerating attitude of gratitude.

1. **Keep a thanksgiving list.** I've been doing this for many years, ever since I read about the British hymnist Frances Ridley Havergal, who kept a thanksgiving list alongside her prayer list. Every morning I

begin my prayer time by listing something for which I'm grateful to the Lord.

2. **Before you fall asleep at night, thank God for three things that happened during the day.** I don't remember where I learned this little technique, but I've been practicing it regularly. In that way, I begin the day with one item of thanksgiving and end it with three. It puts my mind in a better place before it falls asleep.

3. **Keep a thanksgiving journal.** This is the chief tool used by psychologists like Dr. Emmons. They suggest keeping a little notebook in which you write down one, two, or three things each day for which you're thankful.

4. **Give thanks at meals.** We have three opportunities a day to express our thanksgiving to the Lord. You can be specific. "Lord, thank You for this bowl of beans and cornbread." Remember that every good and perfect gift comes down from above, from the Father of lights, from whom there is no shadow or variation (James 1:17).

5. **Whenever you encounter a disappointment or disaster, try to specifically locate and list items for which you can be thankful, even in the midst of the problem.** Write them in your journal, in your calendar, on a sticky note, or in a text to yourself—whatever works to focus your mind on them. The Bible says, "Give thanks in all circumstances; for this is God's will for you in Christ Jesus" (1 Thessalonians 5:18).

6. **Express your gratitude to others.** Let people at work know that you're grateful for their work. Studies have shown that offices are the least common places to hear or express gratitude, and when we express our appreciation to coworkers it increases the overall effectiveness of the organization.[19] The same is true, of course, in home, church, school, and every other social unit.

7. **Read books on gratitude.** I've mentioned a couple of them, and whenever I study a subject or read or listen to a book about it, the subject expands in my mind.

8. **Sing thanksgiving songs and hymns, like "Now Thank We All Our God."** Ephesians 5 tells us to be filled with the Spirit, speaking

to one another with psalms, hymns, and spiritual songs, singing and making melody in our hearts to the Lord, giving thanks always for all things to God the Father in the name of our Lord Jesus Christ (5:18–21). If you're in a difficult place right now, find a song and sing it aloud. It might seem a little awkward, but keep doing it. Find that song online and sing along. It will begin lifting your spirits.

9. **Memorize some thanksgiving passages.** Psalm 100 is a good place to begin. That's the psalm that says, "Enter his gates with thanksgiving and his courts with praise; give thanks to him and praise his name. For the LORD is good and his love endures forever; his faithfulness continues through all generations."

10. **Remember Philippians 4:6, and write out the verse where you can see it.** Underline or capitalize or color or bold or highlight the words, "WITH THANKSGIVING." Make this an undying rule in your life.

Dr. J. Sidlow Baxter recalled a time when, at age eighty-eight, he was asked to speak at a large church in Memphis. He told the group he had been struggling with difficult issues related to his age and health and nerves. He spoke of being on a preaching tour of Scotland when he slumped into a period of deep despondency. "Everything seemed upsetting and frustrating and foreboding."[20] He was also overwhelmed with his workload and shaken by several recent disappointments.

One night, he said:

I went to bed weary with mental wrestling and frustration. And then, somewhere between night and morning, September 6th and 7th, something happened that changed everything. I heard no audible voice, but someone had wakened me amid the curtains of the night; and was speaking within me. By a language which I knew at once. He said, "Sid! Sid! Are you forgetting Philippians 4: verses 6 and 7?" Those verses six and seven perfectly match September six and seven. "You've been forgetting the thanksgiving. Hand everything over to Me, Sid. And start praying again with thanksgiving."[21]

Baxter said:

> I can't explain it too coherently but that is just what I did. In bed, there
> and then, amid the nocturnal darkness I handed everything over to Him.
> And I started praying again with thanksgiving. Somehow I did it with
> ease and then suddenly Philippians 4:6 and 7 was like an electric bulb
> turned on. And I saw everything with illuminating difference and clear-
> ness. My mental tension and gloom had gone.[22]

The next morning Baxter found that his entire nervous system had
become relaxed. "And," he said, "as I prayed with thanksgiving—I could
never forget it—the peace of God invaded my heart like a gentle zephyr."[23]

You and I need the same experience, and it's available from the God of
all peace who gave us these therapeutic steps in Philippians 4:4–7:

> Rejoice in the Lord always.
> Let your gentleness be evident to all.
> The Lord is near.
> Do not be anxious about anything, but in every situation . . . present
> your requests to God.
> With thanksgiving.
> And the peace of God, which transcends all understanding, will guard
> your hearts and minds in Christ Jesus.

DISCUSSION QUESTIONS

1. When we read "with thanksgiving" in Philippians 4 and turn the
   page of our Bibles, we find a list of ways in which we are to live a
   life worthy of God and please Him in every way. Look at Colossians
   1:10–12. What are these three ways, and what role does gratitude
   have in living a God-worthy and God-pleasing life?
2. Consider a crisis you've endured in the past. Did it contain elements,

however small, for which you could express thanksgiving? Were there a few rays of sunlight amid the clouds? What were they? How would your attitude have changed if you had included the concept of "with thanksgiving" into that experience?

3. This chapter suggests ten workable strategies for nurturing a greater habit of thanksgiving. Which habit seems most workable to you? How can you launch this habit today?

CHAPTER SIX

THE PRACTICE OF THINKING

*Whatever is true . . . noble . . . right . . . pure . . . lovely . . .
admirable . . . excellent . . . praiseworthy—think about such things.*

PHILIPPIANS 4:8

I was on a flight to Toronto beside a woman whose nose was in a book. I hunkered down in the window seat with my Bible and notepad and studied through the flight. We didn't chat until time to land, at which point she looked over and commented about my studying the Bible. I told her I enjoyed studying the Bible very much. She told me she was the national director of human resources for a large automotive company, and that she had read her Bible in younger years. On one occasion, she said, she had been asked to give a recitation. She had several choices of material, but she had chosen a passage from the Bible, and it had meant a great deal to her at the time.

"Oh," I said, "what passage did you read?"

"It was from, now, let me see . . . what was it? Fallopians?"

"You mean Philippians?"

"Yes," she said, "Philippians. Maybe it was . . . is there a chapter 4?"

"Was it this passage?" I asked, and then I quoted Philippians 4:4–9 to her, word for word. To my surprise, she grew visibly flustered and emotional.

She broke into tears and started fanning herself with her hands, saying, "I don't know what's happening to me. I'm not usually like this at all."

She hauled up her purse—it was the size of a small Saint Bernard—and began searching for a tissue, which was nowhere to be found. The tears ran down her cheeks and she mopped them up with her palms. I offered my handkerchief.

"I've been so busy and so stressed," she explained, wiping her eyes, "that I've been short with people recently and I've been demanding and difficult and worried. And here you are, quoting something to me I learned long ago and had forgotten. I guess I needed to remember those words again."

By the time she composed herself, we were herded off the plane like cattle, all of us late for connecting flights. I didn't even get the woman's name. But what a blessing to share Philippians 4 with her and to see the effect these simple words had on her thoughts and feelings. She badly needed to refocus her mind on truths she had learned long ago, but which had vanished from her memory like a dissipating mist.

When our minds are overtaken with worry, distress, or discouragement, there's only one thing to do. We have to remember. We have to call to mind the truths we need. We have to take control of our thoughts and stop listening to ourselves and start talking to ourselves. We have to preach to ourselves, lecture ourselves, exhort ourselves. In short, we must go on to the next verse in Paul's prescription for a better life—the practice of thinking. Philippians 4:8 says:

> Finally, brothers and sisters, whatever is true, whatever is noble, whatever is right, whatever is pure, whatever is lovely, whatever is admirable—if anything is excellent or praiseworthy—think about such things.

Out of the thirty-two words in that sentence, only one is an action verb, and it's the key word of the verse and the sole imperative—*think*.

Let's go back to the original hypothesis for this book. In terms of his natural personality, I believe the apostle Paul was, to some degree, a bundle of nervous energy, absorbed in his work, and subject to passionate concern.

His anxiety in Troas had short-circuited his ministry there, though God had opened great doors in that city. But Paul was a devoted student of the Hebrew Scriptures, and it's clear he searched the books and parchments of the Old Testament for a greater acquisition of the peace of God. Perhaps in his studies he came across these words:

> Be careful how you think; your life is shaped by your thoughts. (Proverbs 4:23 GNT)

> You will keep him in perfect peace,
> Whose mind is stayed on You,
> Because he trusts in You. (Isaiah 26:3 NKJV)

> Search me, God, and know my heart;
>   test me and know my anxious thoughts.
> See if there is any offensive way in me,
>   and lead me in the way everlasting. (Psalm 139:23–24)

If we have anxious thoughts we'll be anxious people, because what we *think* is the most important thing about us. We *are* what we *think*, and our lives, attitudes, feelings, reactions, results, failures, successes, and personalities are formed by the strands of thought that tie our brain cells together like baling wire. This is so self-evident it's been at the heart of philosophy and religion from the beginning of human civilization.

Even non-Christians know this. The Hindus taught, "Man becomes that of which he thinks." The Buddha said, "The mind is everything: what you think you become." Marcus Aurelius said, "Your life is what your thoughts make it." Descartes wrote: "I think, therefore I am." The nineteenth-century Unitarian preacher William Channing wrote: "All that a man does outwardly is but the expression and completion of his inward thought."[1]

Ralph Waldo Emerson summed it up nicely, saying, "A man is what he thinks about all day long."[2]

William James laid the foundation for today's motivational movement and positive-thinking literature with these simple words: "The greatest discovery of my generation is that human beings can alter their lives by altering their attitudes of mind."[3]

The homespun British philosopher James Allen wrote:

A man is literally what he thinks, his character being the complete sum of all his thoughts. . . . Good thoughts bear good fruit, bad thoughts bad fruit. . . . Let a man radically alter his thoughts, and he will be astonished at the rapid transformation it will effect in the material conditions of his life. Men imagine that thought can be kept secret, but it cannot; it rapidly crystallizes into habit, and habit solidifies into circumstances.[4]

Allen added, "As the physically weak man can make himself strong by careful and patient training, so the man of weak thoughts can make them strong by exercising himself in right thinking."[5]

That's Paul's point in Philippians 4:8. Many of the men I've just quoted weren't committed to biblical truth, but by sheer deduction they discovered a biblical truth so self-evident it can't be ignored. As Proverbs 23:7 puts it, "For as he thinketh in his heart, so is he" (KJV). This is an inescapable biblical fact, and Philippians 4:8 is one of the Bible's greatest declarations about the power of our thoughts in molding our personalities and moving us into realms of God's peace.

To live more and worry less, we must think and we must think rightly, on the right things, at the right time, on the right wavelengths, with our antenna tuned to the frequency of God's truth. We cannot overcome anxiety unless we learn to replace *worried* thoughts with *worthy* thoughts, thoughts that come directly from the mind of the God of peace. That requires thinking on things that are true, noble, lovely, and praiseworthy.

Thinking is an activity that's fallen on hard times. We're too busy to think, and our minds are congested with noise. It's hard to meditate with our phones clamoring like calliopes, incoming messages arriving like missiles, and headsets blaring like the Tower of Babel.

We don't ride horses into town now. Our work isn't undertaken in quiet fields, disturbed by nothing beyond the murmur of the wind or the distant baying of a dog. We no longer read by the flicker of candlelight or the glow of a fireplace. All that was lost long ago in the Industrial Revolution; now the Information and Technology Revolutions instantly deliver the cacophony of the world straight into our eardrums via a billion speakers and earphones. We rush through traffic like salmon bolting upstream for spawning. We're bombarded by noise and besieged by stimuli. Surround sound is a way of life, and lost to us—without true spiritual effort—is the spirit of Isaiah 30:15: "In quietness and confidence shall be your strength" (NKJV). Or Psalm 46:10: "Be still, and know that I am God."

When we learn to take time for thinking, and when we learn to think in the right way, the benefits come over us like a metamorphosis. This once happened to E. Stanley Jones. Though he had gone to India as a missionary with visionary passion, his energy had evaporated amid unbearable heat, hostility, and anxiety. He collapsed, and even prolonged rest failed to restore him. His nerves were shot. He resembled the apostle Paul at Troas.

One night in the city of Lucknow, while praying, Stanley Jones suddenly felt the Lord speaking to him. Though not audible, the Lord's voice almost seemed so. Jones sensed these words: *Are you yourself ready for this work to which I have called you?*

"No, Lord, I am done for," Jones replied. "I have reached the end of my resources."

The Lord seemed to reply, *If you will turn that over to Me and not worry about it, I will take care of it.*

"Lord," Jones said, "I close the bargain right here." At that moment a great peace settled into his heart and pervaded his whole being:

I knew it was done! Life—Abundant Life—had taken possession of me. I was so lifted up that I scarcely touched the road as I quietly walked home that night. Every inch was holy ground. For days after that I hardly knew I had a body. I went through the days, working far into the night, and came down to bedtime wondering why in the world I should ever go to bed at all, for there was not the slightest trace of tiredness of any kind. I seemed possessed by life and peace and rest—by Christ Himself.[6]

Jones labored on for decades, serving more than forty years in India, preaching around the world—sometimes three times a day, writing a dozen books, and becoming one of the most famous missionaries of his generation. From his evening encounter with the Lord at Lucknow until his death in January 1973, E. Stanley Jones lived in the glow of the sufficiency of Christ Himself, never forgetting the Lord's promise, "If you turn that over to Me and not worry about it, I will take care of it."[7]

If you'll listen quietly and in the stillness of His presence, the Lord is whispering the same words to you. And He tells you to think about such things.

THINK ABOUT SUCH THINGS

Philippians 4:8 is the Bible's great corrective for mindlessness, and the first word says, "*Finally*, brothers and sisters, whatever is true." When the Bible uses the word *finally*, it doesn't necessarily mean we've reached the end of the discussion. It means the discussion is reaching a climactic point. Everything said thus far is leading to the remaining stepping-stones of logic that will fill the subject with fully formed understanding. Sometimes the term is translated "furthermore." In other words, the writer was saying, "Since we have learned the practices of rejoicing, gentleness, nearness, prayer, and thanksgiving, let's proceed to the next level. Let's add the next layer. Let's go on to meditate on things that are true, noble, right, pure, lovely, admirable, excellent, and praiseworthy.

We want to develop minds that migrate, in their most natural and relaxed moments, to thoughts that are:

- True

    Truth is an attribute of God. Everything about Him is absolutely and utterly true, for He is truth. His truth is reflected in everything

He has made throughout His universe. All of creation evidences measurable scientific facts, consistent laws, and immutable principles. Everything God says is utterly true, and every word in the Bible is absolutely and objectively true and trustworthy. These, then, are the things we should think about. These represent where our thoughts should be centered.

- **Noble**

  This is a royal word that conveys the nobility of a king. Sometimes this is translated "honorable," conveying the idea of honor and dignity, good character, worthy of respect. We should train our minds to dwell and daydream on whatever is noble.

- **Right**

  The idea behind this word isn't simply "correct." It conveys the idea of being morally right, all right, upright. Think of it this way: our minds will be either *upright* or *uptight*, but it's hard for them to remain in both conditions for long.

- **Pure**

  In an age of epidemic pornography and immorality, God wants our minds to dwell on things that are pure. In the days of Noah, "The LORD saw how great the wickedness of the human race had become on the earth, and that every inclination of the thoughts of the human heart was only evil all the time" (Genesis 6:5). Only the power of God's true, noble, and right Word can reverse this process in our minds. A steady habit of meditation in His Word day and night is the divine filtration system of the heart that keeps our thoughts pure.

- **Lovely**

  The first four letters of this word spell "love." It refers to the things we love doing, thinking, seeing, or experiencing, things that are beautiful, eloquent, elegant, captivating, and appealing to our highest impulses.

- **Admirable**

  If you can't admire it, don't desire it.

- **Excellent**

  These are God's most outstanding truths. The apostle Paul used this word in Titus 3:8, when he told Titus to teach the true doctrines of Scripture. "I want you to stress these things," Paul wrote, "so that those who have trusted God may be careful to devote themselves to doing what is good. These things are excellent and profitable for everyone."

• Praiseworthy

We should think about the God we praise—and about all the things we can praise Him for. "The highest science, the loftiest speculation, the mightiest philosophy which can ever engage the attention of a child of God is the name, the nature, the person, the work, the doings, and the existence of the great God whom he calls his Father," said Charles Haddon Spurgeon, adding that "there is something exceedingly improving to the mind in a contemplation of the Divinity. It is a subject so vast, that all our thoughts are lost in its immensity; so deep, that our pride is drowned in its infinity."[8]

HOW DO WE THINK ABOUT THESE THINGS?

In a sense, these eight words are a description of God Himself, and of Jesus Christ, who is the epitome of all that is true, noble, right, pure, lovely, admirable, excellent, and praiseworthy. According to 2 Corinthians 3:18, we are transformed by contemplating all He is and all He is for us: "And we all, who with unveiled faces contemplate the Lord's glory, are being transformed into his image with ever-increasing glory, which comes from the Lord, who is the Spirit."

These eight words also describe the scope of Scripture, which brings us back to the habits of Bible study, Scripture memory, and contemplative meditation. Romans 8 says, "Those who live according to the flesh have their minds set on what the flesh desires; but those who live in accordance with the Spirit have their minds set on what the Spirit desires. The mind governed by the flesh is death, but the mind governed by the Spirit is life and peace" (vv. 5–6). Notice the word *peace*. It's the same word we find in

Philippians 4. When our minds are governed by the Spirit and filled with the Scripture, we're training them to move from panic to peace, from worry to worship, and from anxiety to confident trust.

That's why I'm a strong advocate for Scripture memory and meditation. I've written two books on these subjects—*100 Bible Verses Everyone Should Know by Heart* and *Reclaiming the Lost Art of Biblical Meditation*. The patterns I describe in these two books have transformed my life more than anything else I've ever discovered. They've helped me overcome temptation—especially the temptations of distress and discouragement—more than I can describe.

My own habits along these lines are very simple. As I suggested earlier, most mornings during my devotional time I spend a few minutes working on a phrase of a Bible memory verse. It's true we have instantaneous access to Scripture on our phones or tablets, and we can search for a verse with a few taps of a finger. But when we memorize a verse, it gets out of our phones or off of the page of our books, and it's planted in the mental furrows of our conscious minds where it sinks into our subconsciousness—and even into our unconscious thoughts. It's like a radiation chip implanted in our brains that begins working at the deepest levels of our mental functions.

When I decide on a verse to memorize, I write it in a little leather notebook and read it aloud over and over. Taking my phone, I punch the recorder and try quoting the first phrases, then I listen to see what I've missed. I do the same thing the next day. It may take me days, weeks, or even months to learn a passage, but all along the way the passage becomes more familiar. It becomes more deeply etched on the walls of my memory. I often go to sleep thinking about that verse, and I wake up thinking about it, and I think about it in the shower, and I think about it when driving or walking.

Imagine how great this would work for you if you made it your goal to internalize Philippians 4:4–9. Begin by memorizing the first phrase of verse 4: "Rejoice in the Lord always." You can do that. You've probably learned it already just by reading this book. Now add the next phrase: "I will say it again: Rejoice!"

There, now. You've learned a whole verse. You might want to post it on the screen of your phone or with a sticky note to your alarm clock, makeup mirror, or coffeepot. Think about those words as you prepare for the day. Turn them into a prayer as you dress or put the cereal bowl in the dishwasher. *Lord, help me to rejoice in You today.* Turn it into a simple song. Quote it aloud. Say it several times, emphasizing each word in turn. Post it on social media. Share it in correspondence or conversation.

When you feel stressed at work or school, take a one-minute break, find a quiet spot, take several deep breaths, exhaling deeply, inhaling fully, and whisper that verse to yourself. When you get frustrated with your workload, remember the word *always* and say it aloud. Consider Philippians 4:4 as the clothing for your soul today. As you drive home, repeat that sentence several times. Turn it into a prayer for others. "Lord, help my children to rejoice in the Lord this evening." Draw a hot bath, sink into the water, and think of the words of that verse. As you go to sleep, let that thought be the last conscious thing on your mind.

If you get a negative report, hear bad news, or have a panicked moment, say, "Lord, You know I'm tensing up right now, but I'm claiming Philippians 4:4—Rejoice in the Lord always. I will say it again: rejoice!"

You cannot overuse Philippians 4:4 or wear it out or grow tired of it. God's Word is fathomless. I've been thinking about Philippians 4:4 for decades, and I love it more now than when I first learned it. Besides, when you're ready you can add the next phrase: "Let your gentleness be evident to all." Then go on to the next phrase.

Repeat the process verse by verse, and within a few weeks or months you'll have the entire passage stored away in mind, written like calligraphy on your soul, always available, and constantly radiating its truths into the most private places of your heart. Someone sent me a quote that says, "Look around and be distressed. Look within and be depressed. Look above and be at rest." One of the easiest ways of looking above is exploring the heavenly words between the covers of your Bible.

TRANSFORMATIONAL MEDITATION

As you commit to the practice of thinking, you'll soon experience the power of transformational meditation. In my book *Reclaiming the Art of Biblical Meditation*, I recalled a day when I was a freshman at King University in Bristol, Tennessee. A visiting guru with a flowing robe and white beard arrived on campus touting the practice of transcendental meditation. His basic gist, as I recall, was to find moments when we could unwind our muscles, close our eyes, empty our minds, breathe deeply, and relax. I like relaxation and deep breathing, and those are important tools in combating tension and anxiety. When we empty and refill our lungs, we're infusing our bloodstream with God's fresh air, which replenishes our brains, calms our moods, and fortifies our nerves.

But the guru was wrong about emptying one's mind. By definition, *meditation* means "directing the mind to dwell on a certain thought," hopefully something that's true, noble, right, pure, lovely, admirable, excellent, and praiseworthy. I didn't know Philippians 4:8 at the time, but I intuitively felt the swami was misguided. Our minds don't make good vacuum chambers. They need nourishing truth.

The next year I transferred to Columbia International University in Columbia, South Carolina, where someone taught me Romans 12:2, a verse about being transformed by the renewing of our minds. I learned that what God desires for us isn't *transcendental* meditation, but *transformational* meditation.

As we internalize, visualize, and personalize God's Word, we're transformed into the kind of people He wants us to be. We see things from His perspective. We think increasingly as Jesus does, and our minds are deepened, sharpened, composed, and calmed. J. B. Phillips rendered Romans 12:2 like this: "Don't let the world around you squeeze you into its own mould, but let God re-mould your minds from within" (PHILLIPS).[9]

This strategy saved the life of missionary Geoffrey Bull, a Scottish expatriate who was captured and imprisoned by Chinese communists in Tibet. His possessions, including his Bible, were stripped from him and he was thrown into a series of prisons, where he suffered terribly for three years.

In addition to extreme temperatures, scant food, and miserable conditions, Bull was subjected to such mental and psychological torture he feared he would go insane. But he had studied the Bible all his life, so he began to systematically go through Scripture in his mind.

He found it took him about six months to go all the way through the Bible mentally. He started at Genesis, and recalled each incident and story as best he could, first concentrating on the content and then musing on certain points, seeking light in prayer. He continued through the Old Testament, reconstructing the books and chapters as best he could and focusing his thoughts on verses he knew by heart; then into the New Testament and on to Revelation. Then he started over again. He later wrote: "The strength received through this meditation was, I believe, a vital factor in bringing me through, kept by the faith to the very end."[10]

The great thing about internalizing Scripture through memorization and meditation is its power to transform us and even to convert our circumstances and surroundings from anxiety-inducing to praise-producing.

Why not start now with Philippians 4:4–9? Whatever is true, noble, right, pure, lovely, admirable, excellent, and praiseworthy—think about such things.

LET'S GO A STEP FURTHER

After you've learned and internalized Philippians 4:4–9, what then? Well, find another passage, and as the months, years, and decades go by, you'll be weaving your favorite Bible verses into a blanket that will warm your heart and mind as long as you live and will furnish you endless encouragement to pass along to others. The Word of God will become ingrained into your personality like veins of gold.

When I teach this process to a group, I often break it down into eight simple steps.

1. **Passage.** Begin with a passage of Scripture and read it over and over. The other evening I was overcome with stress and fatigue and a sense

94

of confusion, and I turned to Psalm 121, which I had memorized in the King James Version: "I will lift up mine eyes unto the hills, from whence cometh my help. My help cometh from the LORD, which made heaven and earth." I quoted that psalm to myself, looked it up, read it again, and adopted it as my passage for the evening.

2. **Probe.** The second word is *probe*. Having found a passage to settle down in, you need to read it and study it. I often type the passage out, print it, and dissect it using pens and pencils. In the case of Psalm 121, I noticed how the eight verses divide into four natural stanzas of two verses each, and I drew lines between them, noting how the logic of the psalm progresses from stanza to stanza.

3. **Ponder.** Then we ponder the passage. What does this passage mean? What does it mean to me? How would I explain it to someone else if I had the opportunity? How would I teach it, were I asked to lead a Bible study?

4. **Paint.** It's often helpful to paint a mental picture of the passage and use our imaginations to bring Scripture to life. For someone like me who grew up in the Appalachians, it's easy to think about lifting our eyes up to the mountains. I can close my eyes and see the towering peaks, molded and formed by an infinite hand. The same God who made the ancient hills is nearby to establish my peace, settle my soul, and grant His help.

5. **Personalize.** As you can see, the process of pondering and picturing leads to internalizing the passage and making it personal and practical. There's an application in every verse to your life and mine. When we internalize and personalize a promise of Scripture, putting our name on it and standing on its truth, we've found a great antidote for alarm and anxiety.

6. **Pray.** We can also pray the Scripture: "Lord, You have said my help comes from You, the Creator of the soaring hills. Now, here are areas in which I need Your help today . . ."

7. **Practice.** Then you put the passage into practice through trusting and obeying. Psalm 121 ends with the words, "The Lord shall

preserve thy going out and thy coming in from this time forth, and even for evermore" (KJV). That's a great verse to keep in mind as I head out the door to work, or as I return home after a demanding day. I want to practice the awareness of God's watchful care over all my steps.

8. **Preach.** Sooner or later, you'll have an opportunity to preach the passage to others. I don't necessarily mean in a pulpit at church, but in whatever pulpit you have. Remember how I had an opportunity to quote Philippians 4:4–9 to the woman on the plane? The words God gives us become, as it were, our own personal passages and our greatest treasures. We can't help sharing them with our children, friends, family, and with those we meet during the day.

The most powerful way of conducting family devotions, for example, is to naturally share with your children the verses that are currently enriching your life. Deuteronomy 6:6–7 says, "These commandments that I give you today are to be on your hearts. Impress them on your children. Talk about them when you sit at home and when you walk along the road, when you lie down and when you get up."

So that's my formula for meditation: Passage, Probe, Ponder, Paint, Personalize, Pray, Practice, Preach. If you want a simpler scheme, here's one I learned in college. The practice of meditation involves taking a passage of Scripture and *memorizing* it, *visualizing* it, and *personalizing* it. As you do this, your mind is healed by the transforming truth of God's Word and you begin increasingly to think the way God Himself thinks. You begin to look at life from God's point of view. You develop the wisdom from above (James 3:17).[11]

We should constantly have Scripture flowing through our minds like water through a fountain or oil through a machine.

One day while teaching at Liberty University, I had a wonderful conversation about this with my friend Dr. Gary Mathena. He told me of an experience involving his father, and I asked him if I could close this chapter with his story:

One of my dad's heroes in the ministry was an African-American preacher named Manuel Scott. After hearing Dr. Scott preach one evening, my dad had the opportunity to have breakfast with him the next day. As a young preacher, my dad expressed to Dr. Scott how much he was blessed, encouraged, and inspired by his preaching and the truths he was able to extrapolate out of the Scripture. My dad said, "Dr. Scott, it is so evident that you are a spiritual man. How does a man become spiritual? How can I learn to preach with the insights and depth with which you preach?"

Manuel Scott thought for a moment and said, "Well, Harold, when you wake up in the morning spend time reading and thinking about the Word of God and then throughout the day meditate and ruminate on the Word of God all day long. And then before you go to sleep at night allow the Word of God to bathe your heart and mind." Then Dr. Scott paused and reached up to put his thumbs under his red suspenders and said, "If you'll do that, then one of these days, you'll just wake up spiritual!"[12]

That's the simplest way I know to convey the reality of Philippians 4:8. If you want to worry less and live more, put this into practice immediately: "Whatever is true, whatever is noble, whatever is right, whatever is pure, whatever is lovely, whatever is admirable—if anything is excellent or praiseworthy—think about such things."

DISCUSSION QUESTIONS

1. If you battle traumatic stress, what triggers it? If you struggle with occasional anxiety, what thoughts switch it on? Do you think it's really possible to change your feelings by changing your thoughts? What role does our mind have in determining our emotions?
2. The same man wrote both Philippians 4:8 and Romans 12:2.

Read these two verses. Are they saying the same thing? How does Philippians 4:8 accomplish Romans 12:2?

3. Is there a passage or a verse you can begin to memorize? What initial steps can you take today to begin a lifelong habit of Scripture memory and meditation?

CHAPTER SEVEN

THE PRACTICE OF DISCIPLESHIP

*Whatever you have learned or received or heard
from me, or seen in me—put it into practice.*

—PHILIPPIANS 4:9

Some years ago, a Norwegian woman named Marie Monsen was among two hundred passengers traveling by ship across the Yellow Sea off the coast of China. During the wee hours of the morning she heard gunfire and the sounds of conflict. People shouting. Men arguing. Stampeding footsteps. A band of more than fifty pirates seized control of the ship, intent on holding the passengers as hostages.

Marie later described the thoughts that flashed to mind as she realized what was happening:

Just before daylight I heard pistol shots all over the ship, and I knew immediately what we were in for. The words came to me: "This is a trial of your faith." I remember the thrill of joy that went through me at the thought of it. I was immediately reminded of the word that I had been using much in years gone by, in Isaiah 41:10, and I will read it to you as I had been reading it down on the Honan plains, "Fear not, Marie, for I am with thee; be not dismayed, Marie, for I am thy God; I will strengthen thee, Marie, yea, I will uphold thee, Marie, with the right hand of My righteousness."[1]

Marie Monsen had been doing what I prescribed in the last chapter—memorizing and personalizing key passages of Scripture, in this case Isaiah 41:10—and the Holy Spirit brought that verse instantly to her mind. For twenty-three days, she stood on that promise. As she later told the story, the pirates tried to intimidate her, but she wasn't easily unnerved. When they aimed their pistols at her, she told them no weapon formed against her would succeed. When they ordered her into the hold of the ship, she refused to go. When they told her to leave her cabin, she told them God had given her that cabin and she wasn't leaving. When one pirate stole her wristwatch, another returned to it her.[2]

Her cabin was situated between the hijackers' headquarters and the ammunition store, so she had a bird's-eye view of the action as the outlaws used the ship to intercept and raid other vessels, but Marie never lost her sense of peace. Nor was she averse to quoting Scripture to her captors. For three weeks, she took every opportunity of sharing Christ with the passengers and pirates, including the chief, with whom she spent two hours explaining the gospel. Marie was finally released without suffering any harm. The pirates just didn't know what to do with a woman like her.[3]

When I read stories of people like Marie Monsen, it inspires me to be more like them, determined to follow their example. If they trusted Christ in every situation, why shouldn't I? If they found courage in the Lord, so should I! It's humbling to put myself in their places and imagine how differently I might have reacted. I reckon I would have been fearful, panicked, and agitated, but maybe not. The lives of believers through the ages have taught us God imparts grace as we need it, and there's nothing like having worthy models to follow, great mentors to emulate, and heroes to pave the way.

When the writer of the book of Hebrews wanted to encourage his nervous readers to persevere under pressure, he told them, "Now faith is confidence in what we hope for and assurance about what we do not see. This is what the ancients were commended for" (11:1–2). He then listed the examples of Abel, Enoch, Noah, Abraham, and the roll call of Old Testament heroes, who, through faith, conquered kingdoms, shut the mouths of lions, and gained what was promised.

We have two thousand more years of Christian biography to add to that procession, and if we want to strengthen our faith and overcome the armies of anxiety arrayed against us, we need to learn from their examples. If these men and women overcame anxiety, pulled down strongholds, lived boldly for their faith, and gained the reward, so can we. So can our generation.

As we practice rejoicing, gentleness, nearness, prayer, thanksgiving, and meditation, we must add the practice of discipleship. The word *disciple* literally means "learner," and it has to do with following and emulating the teaching and example of another. If we belong to Christ, we're primarily His disciples, but He often uses certain people to spur us on, instruct us, teach us, mentor us, and disciple us in the truths and techniques of our faith. Some of these mentors dwell in yesteryear and cast their shadows over our pathways from afar. Others step right onto our pathway now and come alongside as friends, pastors, counselors, mentors, and teachers. We cannot overcome the anxieties of life without the help of these God-given allies.

This is a lifelong process. Even at so-called retirement age, I need mentors and advisers more than ever. We seldom evolve from anxious fear to unshakable faith in a day or a week, but we can move from weakness to strength by persevering over time, especially when we let others help us. Earlier in Philippians, Paul encouraged his readers by telling them he was confident "that he who began a good work in you will carry it on to completion until the day of Christ Jesus" (1:6).

That involves process and progress.

The psalmist prayed, "The LORD will perfect that which concerns me; Your mercy, O LORD, endures forever" (Psalm 138:8 NKJV), or, as *The Message* puts it, "Finish what you started in me, GOD. Your love is eternal—don't quit on me now."

He won't quit on us, and we must not quit either. Month by month, year by year, and decade by decade, we can have greater calmness and composure, growing as sturdy as oaks with the passing of the seasons. Our anxious nerves can learn to relax in His love, lean on His promises, and trust in His grace. Our peace of mind can overwhelm the baser elements of our personalities. Someone said, "The older you get, the more you become like the place you're going." In Christ, we're headed to an unshakable city prepared for unsinkable souls, so we should learn from others how to be stronger during the journey.

True, we may have regressions along the way. Everyone who battles some variation of traumatic stress knows how our deepest fears can ignite in an instant when triggered by some word, event, sound, smell, or thought. But Proverbs 24:16 says, "The godly may trip seven times, but they will get up again. But one disaster is enough to overthrow the wicked" (NLT). With the examples of Jesus and His followers through all the ages, we have the resources to keep getting up, continuing on, and gaining ground until the Lord takes us home. When it comes to winning over worry, we never give up.

All this brings us to the next verse in our study of Philippians 4 and to the practice of discipleship. In verse 9 Paul said, "Whatever you have learned or received or heard from me, or seen in me—put it into practice. And the God of peace will be with you." Paul had himself battled anxiety, so he knew how to help others find God's peace. In Philippians 4:4–9, he was offering more than a prescription for overcoming anxiety; he was offering himself as living proof of the efficacy of the treatment.

The lesson of verse 9 is quite simple: if you're battling worry and anxiety, find people who know how to trust the Lord better than you, and study their lives. Ask them about faith. Read their stories. Be discipled by their examples. J. B. Phillips translated Philippians 4:9 like this: "Model your conduct on what you have learned from me, on what I have told you and shown you, and you will find the God of peace will be with you" (PHILLIPS).

In presenting himself as a model and mentor, Paul was repeating something he had said earlier in Philippians 3:17: "Join together in following my example, brothers and sisters, and just as you have us as a model, keep your eyes on those who live as we do."

He said something similar in 1 Corinthians 11:1: "Follow my example, as I follow the example of Christ."

That sounds a little audacious, but we have to remember the Christians in Corinth and Philippi didn't have the New Testament as we do. The pastors, elders, and deacons of those days didn't have the full Bible, and the

Gentile converts knew little of the Old Testament. Imagine being a convert in a newly established church, but having little or no Scripture. Bible study wasn't possible, for there were no Bibles. The great Handbook of Holiness, called the New Testament, was still under construction. Perhaps some of the earliest New Testament writings like James and Galatians were beginning to circulate, but they weren't widespread or readily available. Some of Paul's writings were floating through the empire—perhaps 1 Thessalonians, maybe 1 Corinthians. However, the New Testament as we know it was largely unwritten and unassembled, so converts coming in waves across the Roman Empire had few documents to show them how Christians think, act, speak, or live. These first Christians wanted to know: What does a Christian look like? What does a Christian do? How does a Christian act? How is a Christ-follower different from everyone else?

While they didn't have the Bible in print, they did have the biblical culture embodied in the personalities of Paul, Peter, James, John, and the surviving apostolic band. The original followers of Christ exemplified and personified the Christian lifestyle, saying in effect, "If you want to live as a disciple, then watch us. Do what we do. Talk like we talk. Act like we act. Think like we think. Live like we live. Die like we die. Follow our example as we follow Christ. Whatever you have learned or received or heard from us, or seen in us—put it into practice. And the God of peace will be with you."

Today we have the Bible. We have the Old and New Testaments. We have the gospel accounts and the letters and narratives and revelations. Yet we still need models and mentors to help us see how the Word becomes flesh. We need patterns to follow.

If you study the greatest figures in Christian history, you'll always find a mentor behind them. The history of Christianity is the story of disciples mentoring disciples, from generation to generation, from one era to the next, in an endless chain of transformation (2 Timothy 2:2).

When he was a young man, for example, Martin Luther had a mentor named Johann von Staupitz, the leader of the Augustinian community in Munich. Luther was an anxious and conflicted young monk, but Von Staupitz taught him to look to Christ and wait on God's grace through prayer, not striving in his own efforts. Von Staupitz prompted Luther to study the book of Romans—a suggestion that changed history through the Reformation.

Consider the statesman William Wilberforce, whose lifelong campaign against human trafficking ended commercial slavery in the British Empire. As a child, Wilberforce listened to the sermons of John Newton, the author of the hymn "Amazing Grace." Newton had been the captain of a slave ship before his conversion to Christ. Now he was a pastor and a great opponent of slavery.

The course of circumstances moved Wilberforce away from Newton's influence, and, as a teenager and young adult, the future statesman didn't have a strong Christian presence in his life. Indeed, he himself was not a Christian. But after being elected to Parliament at age twenty-one, Wilberforce was dramatically converted to Christ and wavered about staying in politics. He worried that the political world wasn't compatible with Christian values. He sought out his old pastor, John Newton, who encouraged him to remain in the government to advance the cause of Christ in the political arena and to strive for the abolition of slavery.

In the years that followed, many people vilified Wilberforce and he often became anxious and stressed. At such times, he would confide in his mentor. On July 21, 1796, for example, Wilberforce wrote to Newton, disclosing his thoughts of retiring from public life. Newton wrote back:

> You meet with many things which weary and disgust you, which you would avoid in a more private life. But then they are inseparably connected with your path of duty; and though you cannot do all the good you wish for, some good is done, and some evil is probably prevented by your influence . . . It costs you something . . . and exposes you to many impertinences from which you would gladly be exempted; but if, upon the whole, you are thereby instrumental in promoting the cause of God and the public good, you will have no reason to regret. . . .
>
> Nor is it possible at present to calculate all the advantages that may result from your having a seat in the House at such a time as this. The

example, and even the presence of a consistent character may have a powerful, though unobserved, effect upon others. You are not only a representative for Yorkshire, you have the far greater honour of being a representative for the Lord, in a place where many know Him not.[4]

Newton ended his letter by reminding Wilberforce of the example of the statesman and prophet Daniel who served in the courts of Babylon:

> It is true that you live in the midst of difficulties and snares, and you need a double guard of watchfulness and prayer. But since you know both your need of help, and where to look for it, I may say to you as Darius to Daniel, "Thy God whom thou servest continually is able to preserve and deliver you." Daniel, likewise, was a public man, and in critical circumstances; but he trusted in the Lord, was faithful in his department, and therefore, though he had enemies, they could not prevail against him.
>
> Indeed the great point for our comfort in life is to have a well grounded persuasion that we are where, all things considered, we ought to be.[5]

Notice how John Newton mentored Wilberforce back to the biblical model of Daniel, and in so doing gave him an example of a man who, in similar governmental straits, kept calm and carried on. We, too, can learn to withstand the pressures of anxiety by practicing discipleship as it relates to biblical models, examples in Christian biography, and contemporary friends and mentors whose lives show us how to better trust the Lord. In other words, if you're beset by worry, find someone who isn't and learn their secret.

It's this practice of discipleship and mentoring that occupies Philippians 4:9, and according to this verse, we can tap into a fourfold influence. Notice the key verbs: "Whatever you have *learned* or *received* or *heard* from me, or *seen* in me—put it into practice." The Bible doesn't waste words, so each of those terms gives us a different way in which we can mentor or be mentored. Discipleship, in other words, occurs on four tracks: through life-changing lessons, life-changing writings, life-changing sermons, and life-changing examples.

WHAT YOU HAVE LEARNED

First, Paul said, "What you have *learned* from me," and this refers to the *life-changing lessons* God teaches us through those He sends across our paths. For Paul and the Philippians, it went back to Acts 16 and the story of the beginnings of the church in Philippi. The very first convert, Lydia, a successful business owner, came to Christ as Paul preached by the riverside. There was a slave girl from whom Paul cast out a demon, resulting in the arrest and persecution of Paul and Silas, who were flogged and imprisoned. Even these events turned for good, for as the missionaries sang at midnight, God sent an earthquake and set them free. The jailer and his family subsequently placed their faith in Christ, and these several souls became the firstfruits of the harvest in Philippi. Now, years later in his letter, Paul wanted to show them how, by following his example, they could experience transcendent peace.

As I reflect on my life, I'm grateful for fellow believers who have modeled biblical truth for me and taught me the principles of Scripture—my parents, my childhood pastor Winford R. Floyd, my professors, a handful of upperclassmen at Columbia International University, and a band of brothers and sisters God has brought into my life along the way.

In our book *The Strength You Need*, my wife, Katrina, wrote about the woman who mentored her in Palm Beach, Florida—Antoinette Johnson. Her influence shaped Katrina's life and set her on a new course of growth—without which she and I would never have met.

And speaking of Katrina, no one has helped me more than she in grappling with my anxieties. "I don't know why you're so worried," she has often told me. "You act as though God can't do anything about this. Why don't you just trust Him?"

"I'm trying to trust," I sometimes say.

"*Trying* and *trusting* are opposites," is her invariable response.

These are life-changing lessons of faith we can learn from others.

I've also been fortunate as a pastor to always have governing boards whose hearts were invested in me and in our joint work. The unity and strength of our church leaders have sustained us for forty years. We've occasionally faced difficult days, but I've never had a governing team that crumbled under anxiety. We've persevered together, encouraging each other in faith. Every pastor needs such teams of deacons, elders, leaders, and boards.

Ian Maclaren wrote of a church in Drumtochty, Ireland, where John Carmichael had just begun his ministry. Carmichael was a young man who worked hard on his sermons, but Sunday after Sunday they fell apart as he tried to preach them.

One Sunday after the service when everyone had left, Carmichael remained in the church, feeling dejected. He was sitting alone in the vestry, chin on his chest, when he heard a knock at the door. It was the most senior elder in the church, Angus Sutherland. John braced himself, thinking he was about to be discharged.

"It is good weather we're having, sir," Angus began, speaking English with a soft Gaelic accent. "Maybe I should not be troubling you at this time, but I have been sent by the elders with a message."

The old man told John that the elders had conducted an impromptu meeting under the old beech tree after the service, and he had been sent to convey their decision. He said he came as a friend, and he reminded the young man how the church had taken a chance in hiring such a young pastor.

Then old Angus said in his quaint Scottish style, "It has been three months since you entered upon your ministry among us, and you will not be angry with me if I am saying to you that you are very young to have so heavy a weight upon you, for there is no burden like the burden for souls." He went on to say no one doubted the young man's sincerity or his hard efforts. "But you are very young and the ministry of the Lord is very arduous."

He paused, then continued:

So the elders considered that the full time had come for their saying something to you, and I was charged by them all to wait upon you in this place and to say unto you, on behalf of the elders of the flock and all the flock which is under your care, that we are all thankful unto God that He sent you to be our minister, and are all full of wonder at the treasures of truth and grace which you will be bringing to us every Sabbath.

He continued:

There is just one other thing that the brethren laid upon me to say. We will ask you to remember when you stand in your place to speak to us in the name of the Lord, that as the smoke goeth up from the homes of the people in the morning, so will their prayers be ascending for their minister; and as you look down upon us before you begin to speak, maybe you will say to yourself, next Sabbath, they are all loving me. Oh, yes, and it will be true from the oldest to the youngest, we will all be loving you very much.[6]

No wonder John Carmichael remained in the ministry all his life. The lesson he learned from his elder that Sunday afternoon helped him conquer his nerves, overcome his fears, and persevere in the work for a lifetime.

Whatever your age or stage in life, God has put someone in your life—or soon will—who can mentor you from a life of anxious care into a life of productive peace. God can bring someone into your life who can take you deeper into the life of faith with life-changing lessons, even as Paul said, "Whatever you have learned from me, put it into practice—and the God of peace will be with you."

WHAT YOU HAVE RECEIVED

We're also discipled into peace by *life-changing writings*. Notice how Philippians 4:9 unfolds: "Whatever you have . . . *received* . . . from me . . . put it into practice." What had they received from Paul? His notes, letters, and written teachings, such as the book of Philippians. The entire letter to the Philippians was an exercise in mentoring. And whenever we read Philippians, Paul is still mentoring. He is mentoring us. God is mentoring us through the inspired words He breathed out in Paul's epistle.

This is mentoring through reading. I've never met many of my best mentors; in fact, most of them are dead. But they dwell on the shelves of my library or in my e-reader. Sometimes when I open a book, even in the deepest of night, I feel I'm entertaining its author, whether Aurelius, Augustine, Blaise Pascal, John Bunyan, Thomas Watson, Brother Lawrence, Charles Spurgeon, A. T. Pierson, A. W. Tozer, C. S. Lewis, or whoever's name is on the cover. We've had wonderful times together, just between our shelves, and some of these mentors and their books have changed my life, my thinking, and my attitudes. They've empowered me to grow in my faith and to better cope with my anxieties. You might call it biblio-therapy.

J. I. Packer's *Knowing God* became one of the greatest mentoring forces for my generation, and I still keep a copy on the shelf by my desk. Actually, it's Katrina's copy, which is all marked up. I don't know what happened to mine, but some of the truths in *Knowing God* have seeped by natural osmosis from Packer's book into this one. That's what happens to great books. They soak into our minds and are diffused into our conversations and writings. I've never been able to have a chat with Dr. Packer, but his writings have packed many a punch as I've read them.

I never met Charles Spurgeon; he died sixty years before I was born. But his *Lectures to My Students* crossed my path, and I became Spurgeon's student through his book.

I've never met Chattanooga psychologist Ross Campbell, but his book *How to Really Love Your Child* helped me become a better parent when I first became a father many years ago.

When it comes to worry and anxiety, I've often sought refuge in books like *Spiritual Depression: Its Causes and Cures* by Martyn Lloyd-Jones; *Prescription for Anxiety* by Leslie D. Weatherhead, whose sermons helped postwar London recover its nerves; *God's Cure for Anxious Care* by John R. Rice; *How to Stop Worrying and Start Living* by Dale Carnegie; and—don't judge me—a handful of practical, positive-thinking books by popular authors.

It's possible to read our way to greater peace of mind if we read the right books—starting with the Bible. In the books we read, the sages of the ages become our mentors. Think of it this way: What if you could invite Paul of Tarsus to have a cup of coffee with you? What if you could have tea with G. K. Chesterton? What if Billy and Ruth Graham had an hour to spend with you? D. L. Moody? Fanny Crosby? Jonathan Edwards? Francis Schaeffer? That's the power of reading, and that's why Paul said, "Whatever you have . . . received . . . from me . . . put it into practice. And the God of peace will be with you."

WHAT YOU HAVE HEARD

He also said, "Whatever you have . . . *heard* from me . . . put it into practice. And the God of peace will be with you." He was referring to his oral teachings, lectures, conversations, and *life-changing sermons*. There is electrifying power in the public reading and exposition of God's Word.

When I was a freshman in college, being very immature, discontent, and lukewarm, I happened to turn on the radio in my aunt Louise's living room. She had a huge radio and television console, and every night a station in North Carolina broadcasted a sermon from a Bible conference somewhere in the country. That evening, a British speaker was preaching about the donkey Jesus rode into Jerusalem. That donkey was made for a purpose, said the preacher, and it was standing in a place where two ways met, in the right place and at the right time. Jesus needed him, and that little donkey fulfilled its destiny by serving the Lord. The speaker said, "If God can do something with that donkey, maybe He can do something with you."

That preacher might as well have jumped through the radio and grabbed me by the collar. I felt he was talking personally to me. That was the beginning of the road that presently led me to yield my life to the Lord in full surrender.

In college, it was the lectures of James (Buck) Hatch that laid the foundation for my whole approach to understanding and teaching the Bible. Truth be told, I still go back and listen to his recorded lectures, which I first heard forty years ago.[7]

There's a thought blowing like a stray leaf through church auditoriums today that the most effective sermons are those with the least Scripture. Some preachers habitually preach on the moral or practical themes of

Scripture while avoiding digressions into what the Bible actually says or unfolding the logic of Scripture as it appears. But Psalm 119:130 says, "The unfolding of your words gives light." The act of preaching or teaching isn't simply proclaiming our thoughts about what the Bible says. It's the act of unfolding the words themselves, preaching Scripture progressively, verse by verse, in a way that reflects the logic God wove into the Bible. In Philippians 4:4–9, for example, one sentence follows another in rational order, giving us a wonderful passage to study in its context—and therein lies its power.

When you find a solid Bible expositor, read and study his or her scriptural insights, for as you understand the unfolding logic of God's Word, you'll be better armed to deal with life's perils and alarms.

WHAT YOU HAVE SEEN

Finally, Paul said, "Whatever you have . . . *seen* in me—put it into practice. And the God of peace will be with you." This brings us full circle to the *life-giving examples* that strengthen our faith and reduce our fear as we observe them. Some in the first century never sat down and talked with the apostle Paul. Some never read his letters. Perhaps they didn't have a chance to hear him speak, teach, or preach. But they watched him from afar. He was able to mentor them without ever speaking a word. They saw the expression on his face. They saw the disciplines in his life. They saw the hope in his eyes. They heard about his enthusiasm even amid suffering, and they understood he wasn't a man easily rattled. His life was anchored to hope in Christ. "And because of my chains," he said in Philippians 1:14, "most of the brothers and sisters have become confident in the Lord and dare all the more to proclaim the gospel without fear."

The very presence of people of faith has enormous impact on those who cross their paths. One of the women I wish I'd met was Dr. Henrietta Mears, who served on the staff of a California church in the 1940s, but whose ministry covered the world and whose influence touched countless lives over the years. In his book on revival, Bill Bright talked about a life-changing evening in 1947. He said:

I was in a meeting at Forest Home Christian Conference in California. A dear friend of mine, Dr. Henrietta Mears, director of Christian education at the First Presbyterian Church of Hollywood, was the speaker. Dr. Louis Evans Jr., the son of the senior pastor, and I walked her back to her cabin. We were chatting and enjoying our fellowship, so she invited us in. As we continued to talk, suddenly the Holy Spirit enveloped us. As a young believer, I did not know very much about the person of the Holy Spirit, so I did not know what was happening to me. But I found myself intoxicated with joy. Dr. Evans said it was as though coals of fire ran up and down his spine.

While we were in prayer and praising God, Dr. Richard Halverson entered Dr. Mears's cabin. He was a defeated, frustrated, fruitless Presbyterian minister from Coalinga, California. He had come to seek her counsel on how he might leave the ministry and return to the Hollywood entertainment world from which he had come before his conversion.

When he walked into the room, we were praying and no one said anything to him. But instantly the Holy Spirit healed him of his defeat and frustration, and his heart was filled with joy and love.

In moments we were all changed. None of us was ever the same again, and God gave each of us major responsibilities in His vineyard. Dr. Evans went on to become a nationally-known Presbyterian minister. For many years he pastored the National Presbyterian Church, "the church of the presidents." Dr. Halverson became chaplain of the U.S. Senate.[8]

And Bill Bright? He went on to establish Campus Crusade for Christ, now known as Cru, which became one of the greatest evangelistic forces of the twentieth century, one that still continues in 191 countries.

Henrietta Mears didn't cause that moment of revival in her cabin; the Holy Spirit did. As I've read her biographies, however, I've noticed that moments like that seemed to happen when she was around. Oh, how we want our own lives to radiate revival and to encourage others to wait upon the Lord, to mount up with wings like eagles, and to overcome the lower climates of fear, worry, anxiety, discouragement, and defeat.

That brings us back to our passage and topic. The real subject isn't simply the general practice of discipleship, but the specific kind of discipleship that revamps us into replicas of Christ, whose peace transcends understanding.

Remember, Paul wrote Philippians from prison, and he knew the Philippians were anxious about him. They were anxious about themselves amid the hostility of the Roman Empire. Indeed, they were worried about the very survival of Christianity in the Roman world. There was opposition. There was persecution. Their hero had been incarcerated. But throughout the book of Philippians, Paul was calm. He was cheerful. He was optimistic. He was content. He was joyful and excited.

His message: Be like me! Rejoice in the Lord always as I am doing. Let your gentleness be evident to all as I'm trying to do. Don't forget the Lord is near you as He is near me. Learn to do what I am doing—don't be anxious about anything, but in everything by prayer and petition, with thanksgiving, present your requests to God. Imitate me, and think about whatever is true, noble, right, pure, lovely, and admirable. Whatever you have learned or received or heard from me or seen in me—put into practice.

In order to bury worry before worry buries you, find someone else with a shovel in their hand, who, by faith, is already putting their anxious cares six feet under. It may be a friend, a grandparent, a writer, a pastor, or a senior saint, someone whose face reflects the peace you need. Get to know them. Learn from them. Talk with them if possible and pray with them. Ask them, "How did you learn to trust the Lord as you do?"

And as you follow their example, you'll begin to notice others—whether on a pirate ship or in a mountain cabin—looking to you for their strength in life. And you can tell them, "Whatever you have learned or received or heard from me, or seen in me—put it into practice. And the God of peace will be with you."

This is the practice of discipleship.

DISCUSSION QUESTIONS

1. Name one or two people who had the greatest influence on you as mentors. Why were they so important and what did you learn most from them?
2. Compare 2 Timothy 2:1–2 with John 17:20. What role can you play in this chain of transmission? How does that relate to Matthew 29:19?
3. Think of someone—a child, grandchild, student, friend, or even a stranger—whom you could see yourself influencing, given the opportunity. Who is it? Are there any steps you can take to spur along the process? What are they?

CHAPTER EIGHT

THE PRACTICE OF PEACE

*And the peace of God, which transcends all understanding,
will guard your hearts and your minds in Christ
Jesus. . . . And the God of peace will be with you.*

—PHILIPPIANS 4:7, 9

The inimitable Puritan writer Thomas Watson said, "If God be our God . . . He will give us peace in trouble. When there is a storm without, He will make music within. The world can create trouble in peace, but God can create peace in trouble."[1]

The Prince of Preachers agreed. In one of his matchless sermons, delivered on Sunday, August 3, 1890, Charles Spurgeon, fifty-seven, who was celebrating his fortieth year as a Christian but who was ill and would be dead within two years, told his congregation if they had inner peace they would "dread no outward disturbance, and feel no inward storm—who does not desire such a state?"

His text that morning was Psalm 29:11: "The LORD blesses his people with peace." Waxing eloquent, Spurgeon spoke of the thoughts that had come into his mind the previous evening while meditating on this text:

> As I turned my text over last night, it seemed to me to be a very wonderful passage. . . . "The Lord will bless His people with peace." We have had

peace with God these forty years; yes, but we have a promise of peace for today. Suppose we should live another forty years, we shall still have the same promise—"The Lord will bless His people with peace."

I should like an everlasting check from some millionaire, running thus: "So often as this check is presented at the bank, pay the bearer what he asks." Few persons possessed of such a document would fail to put in an appearance at the bank. We should be regular visitors. Oh, children of God, we have such a promissory note in the text before you! The Lord hath endless, boundless peace within Himself, and when you have long enjoyed peace with Him you may go to Him again and say, "Lord, renew my peace. I am troubled, but Thou art unmoved. Bless me with peace."

When you are rich . . . when you are poor. . . . When children are born to you . . . if the children die. . . . If you grow sick. . . . When you must go upstairs and lie down upon your last bed to rise no more, then, even then, the Lord will bless you with His ever-living peace; and when you wake up at the sound of the last trump, the Lord will still keep you in perfect peace. . . . The Lord will bless His people with peace.

Take this truth home to your heart, and live upon it, and you may dwell perpetually in the presence of the King.[2]

According to our passage in Philippians 4, as we practice the instructions laid out in verses 4–9, our susceptibility to surging worry will recede and we'll find ourselves facing the pressures of our problems with less panic and greater peace—transcendent peace. On occasions that tempt us to feel anxious, we can simply take a deep breath, close our eyes a moment, and mentally make our way through this passage, putting each element into place, one verse at a time.

The result is guaranteed. As we do this consistently, the power of these ancient words will overhaul our minds like an engineer renovating an engine, until all of our thoughts, feelings, and reactions vibrate with peace. Somehow in His infinite grace, God reduces our fears and replaces them with a peace that transcends all understanding. Marvelous peace. Perfect peace. Multiplied peace.

The concept of multiplied peace was a great encouragement to the disabled hymnist Annie Johnson Flint. Her classic poem "He Giveth More Grace" speaks of how God multiplies peace amid multiplied trials and how He gives more grace when our strength is low, when our resources are depleted, and when our labors increase. "He giveth, and giveth, and giveth again," she said.[3]

I have a friend—Karen Singer—whose uncle, Hubert Mitchell, set Annie Johnson Flint's poem "He Giveth More Grace" to music. In the 1930s, Hubert was the music director for noted evangelist Paul Rader. One day in a pastor's office Hubert saw the words of this poem on a plaque, and, personally moved, he composed a wonderful melody for them and turned the popular poem into a beloved hymn that speaks of how God multiplies peace to us.

Hubert Mitchell didn't just put "He Giveth More Grace" to music; he put the words into practice. If God's multiplied peace can sustain us at home, Mitchell pondered, why not overseas? Why not wherever God takes us?

Feeling God's call to Indonesia, Hubert and his wife, Helen, traveled to the island of Sumatra in 1935 to share the message of God's peace, and they had some astonishing adventures. On one occasion, for example, Hubert and his coworkers plunged into the island's interior to search for the elusive Kubus, a tribe of aboriginals. It was a rigorous trip through thick and dangerous jungles, but one evening they broke into a clearing and found a Kubu settlement.

The village women and children ran away, having never before seen a white man. The warriors surrounded the missionaries with spears and poison-tipped blowguns. But when the missionaries explained their purpose, the Kubus welcomed them warmly and Hubert was taken to the chief's hut to spend the night.

The next morning, the village assembled to hear what Hubert had to say. The missionary opened his Indonesian Bible to John 19 and began to read about the death of Christ. He explained who Jesus was, and slowly went through the story of the Lord's crucifixion. At one point, the chief raised his hand and asked, "What is a cross?"

Hubert went to the edge of the clearing, cut down two large saplings, stripped off their branches, and lashed them together to form a cross. He placed the cross on the ground and laid down on it, stretching his arms along the beam.

"But how could a man die, lying there upon two trunks of trees?" asked the chief.

"He was crucified," said Hubert. "They drove sharp nails into His hands and feet."

"What is a nail?" asked the chief.

Hubert struggled to describe a nail. He ransacked his duffle bag looking for anything resembling a nail, but came up empty. He could see the villagers losing interest in the story, and some began drifting away. It was time for lunch, so the meeting broke up and Hubert went down to the stream and prayed, saying, "Please, Lord, give me some way to explain a nail to these people."

Someone handed him a banana leaf, filled with rice and dried fish, and afterward Hubert reached into his knapsack and took out a can of mandarin oranges for dessert. The oranges, which Hubert purchased in a Chinese store near his home base, had been canned in Japan. Opening the oranges, he poured them into a dish and was about to throw away the can when he heard a rattling sound. There, to his amazement, was a shiny, new, three-inch nail. It had been hermetically sealed in the can, perfectly preserved with the oranges.

"Look!" he shouted. "This is a nail! This is what they used to nail Jesus to the cross." The chief ran over and took the nail from Hubert's hand. He felt its sharp point against his palm. As the tribe reassembled, Hubert continued the story of Jesus, His death and resurrection, and the people were totally absorbed by the message. They begin crying, "How great the love of God! How great the love of God!" One by one, the members of the Kubu tribe confessed Christ as Savior and were baptized in the nearby stream. These new believers began going to other tribes with the same message, and in this way the gospel spread through central Sumatra.

According to Hubert Mitchell's niece, Karen, who attends our church in Nashville, his story was one of sacrifice and stress, but he lived out the concept of multiplied peace. The Lord imparted grace to him, giving it over and over and over again. To multiplied trials, God multiplied peace.[4]

I love the premise of "more grace" and "multiplied peace," because that's what I so badly need. The God of miracles, who can drop nails into cans of sliced oranges, can hammer His peace into our hearts. He doesn't just *add* peace to our lives, but He drives it in, nailing it down, magnifying it, multiplying it. The Bible's answer to anxiety and worry is spelled p-e-a-c-e.

Here in Philippians 4, the Lord presents this to us in two ways: in verse 7, we read about the *peace of God*, and in verse 9, we encounter the *God of peace*.

THE PEACE OF GOD

The first part of the passage talks about the peace of God. Let's review Philippians 4:4–6 and remind ourselves of the sequence of thought in these verses. To worry less and live more, we begin by consciously and intentionally taking control of our perspective, aggressively adopting an attitude of joy (verse 4). That allows us to bring a gentler spirit to our personalities (verse 5). As we remember the Lord is near (verse 5), we're able to pray, to cast our cares on Him in every situation (verse 6), and to identify those elements of our circumstances for which we can be thankful (verse 6).

Now, in verse 7, God makes a pledge to us. When we consciously and actively do those things, there will be a tremendous outcome. Those habits will produce a reality in our lives no amount of money can purchase, something that has eluded the presidents, prime ministers, and premiers of history. We will become recipients of something so powerful and pervasive it will forever change our lives, our personalities, our legacies—everything about us.

And the peace of God, which transcends all understanding, will guard your hearts and your minds in Christ Jesus.

Just as we've studied Philippians 4:4–9 in a progressive way, looking at one verse after another, we must do the same with this verse, looking at every word in consecutive order. The first words tell us the origin of peace: *"And the peace of God."* This kind of peace is God's kind of peace, His own impregnable volume of calmness. His own unlimited measure of composure—strong, deep, fathomless, unshakable, impregnable, and grounded in eternal hope. It is the serenity of the Trinity—derived from the Father, purchased for us by the Son, installed in our hearts and instilled within our minds by the Holy Spirit.

God never feels a worried moment. He dwells above all the cares of the world, inhabiting eternity and occupying infinity. He knows the end from the beginning. No threat can disturb Him and no foe can threaten Him; for He—He alone—is the Creator, Sustainer, and Commander of the universe and all it contains. He is the Ruler of all reality, in all realms, in all epochs and ages, whether seen or unseen, whether visible or invisible. His infinite power merges with limitless love to reassure His people of His obstinate providence. He can replace your transient worries with transcendent peace.

Because God is infinite, His measureless peace is never exhausted, nor even diminished, regardless of its outflow. Because He is unchanging, His peace is unwavering. Because He is almighty, His peace is all-powerful, fully able to pull down the strongholds of anxiety in our lives. Because He is omnipresent, His peace is available to every one of us, everywhere, on every occasion, in every location, wherever we find ourselves. Because He is all-knowing, His peace is astute, perceptive, and unerring. Because God is faithful, His peace is steadfast.

Philippians 4:7 goes on to describe it this way: "And the peace of God, *which transcends all understanding."*

In other words, the peace of God defies all attempts to describe, analyze, explain, or comprehend it. This is the peace that God Himself possesses within the infinity of His attributes. It's the peace that flows from Him like currents in the ocean and streams in the desert, and it is transcendent. When I first became acquainted with this passage, I was using the King James Version, which uses the phrase "And the peace of God, which passeth all understanding." The word Paul used means "to surpass, to transcend, to exceed, to go beyond, to rise above, to be overarching, and to arc around."

Let's use all these synonyms and create our own expanded paraphrase of the verse: "And the peace of God, which surpasses, exceeds, transcends, goes beyond, rises above, and arcs around all human understanding—that is the peace that will guard your hearts and minds."

In Ephesians 3:19, Paul used similar terminology about the love of God, when he wrote that God's love "surpasses knowledge." Just think! In Philippians 4:7, we have the peace of God that transcends understanding; in Ephesians 3:19, we have the love of God that surpasses knowledge.

What multiplied gifts from Him who gives more grace!

The next phrase in the verse tells us what this incredible peace does for us: "And the peace of God, which transcends all understanding, *will guard . . .*" The word Paul used in the original Greek is a military term for a contingent of solders assigned to protect someone. It's a word that implies having a bodyguard or a protective force around you. Security services speak of creating bubbles or perimeters around their clients, and if the client is a head of state, there may be concentric protective perimeters around them wherever they go.

The peace of God isn't just a warm feeling of well-being or an ephemeral emotion. It's as tough as a soldier, as tenacious as a marine, as stalwart as a seaman, as adamant as an airman. It's God's Special Forces, arrayed like a bodyguard stationed at the entrance of your thoughts and your emotions—your heart and your mind—to protect and keep you.

Notice how Paul mentions both heart and mind: "And the peace of God, which transcends all understanding, will guard *your hearts and your minds.*"

When it comes to worry and anxiety, there is both a mental and an emotional aspect to them. It is impossible to chart the border between our thoughts and feelings, for they are intertwined like threads in embroidery. But we know from experience how our minds and our hearts bear our concerns differently. Sometimes I have more trouble with a worried mind when my problems barge in and commandeer my thoughts. On other occasions, my nerves are edgy, and I experience feelings of uneasiness, even when my mind struggles to pinpoint the source of my worry. My thoughts give me headaches, and my feelings give me stomachaches.

That's why the God of peace sends two detachment of soldiers to help—one to compose our minds with truth and the other to guard our emotions with trust. As J. B. Phillips translates it: "The peace of God which transcends human understanding, will keep constant guard over your hearts and minds as they rest in Christ Jesus" (PHILLIPS).

In an earlier chapter, I suggested Paul had drawn the principles of Philippians 4 from his own study of the Hebrew Scriptures—the Old Testament. Here's another example. Philippians 4:7 has its roots in Isaiah 26:3–4, which says, "You will keep in perfect peace those whose minds are steadfast, because they trust in you. Trust in the LORD forever, for the LORD, the LORD himself, is the Rock eternal."

Notice the parallels between Isaiah 26:3–4 and Philippians 4:7. God Himself is our source of peace, and the peace is indescribable—a perfect peace (*shalom, shalom*), a peace that transcends human understanding. Likewise, in Isaiah 26, the word *keep* conveys the idea of a military guard stationed around the steadfast mind, the mind that is stayed on Jehovah and founded on an unshakable Rock.

Isaiah later compared the peace of God to a river flowing through the soul (Isaiah 66:12), and hymnist Frances Havergal combined the pictures to give us a visual portrait of God's peace:

> *Like a river glorious is God's perfect peace,*
> *Over all victorious, in its bright increase;*
> *Perfect, yet it floweth, fuller ever day,*
> *Perfect, yet it growth, deeper all the way.*
> *Stayed upon Jehovah, hearts are fully blest,*
> *Finding, as He promised, perfect peace and rest.*[5]

I especially love Havergal's second verse, which says when we're hidden in God's perfect hand no foe can follow and no traitor stand:

Not a surge of worry, not a shade of care,
Not a blast of hurry touch the spirit there.[6]

That brings us to the last phrase of Philippians 4:7: "And the peace of God, which transcends all understanding, will guard your hearts and your minds *in Christ Jesus*." When you study this subject of peace throughout the Bible, the most consistent fact is its connection with Jesus Christ. Years ago, this was popularized on church signs by the slogan: "Know Christ, Know Peace. No Christ, No Peace." Perhaps the phrasing is trite, but the truth is inescapable when one studies the subject of peace in the Scriptures.

- In Isaiah 9:6, the Messiah is called the "Prince of Peace."
- In Isaiah 53:5, we read, "He was pierced for our transgressions, he was crushed for our iniquities; the punishment that brought us peace was on him."
- When Jesus was born in Bethlehem, the angels proclaimed "peace on earth" (Luke 2:14).
- The book of Acts says the message of the gospel is "the good news of peace through Jesus Christ" (Acts 10:36).
- Romans 5:1 says, "Therefore, since we have been justified through faith, we have peace with God through our Lord Jesus Christ."
- Ephesians 2:14 says, "For he himself is our peace."

Additionally, Jesus said in John 14:27, "Peace I leave with you; my peace I give you. I do not give to you as the world gives. Do not let your hearts be troubled and do not be afraid." Those were among Christ's final words as He met with His disciples in the Upper Room on the eve of His crucifixion. He gave them His last will and testament.

How many times have we watched television shows in which families gather for the reading of someone's last will? We wait in suspense to see who will be millionaires and who will be paupers. In John 14:27, Jesus issued His will. He didn't have property or houses to leave; He didn't even have a pillow for His head. He didn't have money; Judas Iscariot had absconded with our Lord's last shekel. He couldn't leave His clothing; His executioners would divide that among themselves. But He did have one thing to leave His disciples—His perfect, transcendent, unassailable peace.

How tragic when we fail to claim our inheritance! When we live in anxiety and frantic worry when Jesus Christ, in the last hours of His life, bestowed on us the legacy of His own peace. Nothing could be more beneficial to your heart and mind than to memorize John 14:27, alongside Philippians 4:4–6. Learn these verses well and ponder them often, so the Holy Spirit can bring them to your mind and apply them to your heart during the rough patches of life.

I had a friend in college named Scott Burlingame. He married a wonderful woman named Joyce, and they devoted their lives to ministry. While Scott was serving as a pastor in Columbia, South Carolina, he was diagnosed with cancer, and the news went from bad to worse. Scott's illness proved terminal. During their months on this journey, Joyce sent prayer updates to friends, and these updates read like journal entries. After Scott's death, she compiled them in a book entitled *Living with Death, Dying with Life*. One of her entries was dated January 17, 2011:

> These are truly hard days. Although Scott can eat just a little, it is not much. I am carefully trying to add new foods, but then find we are back where we started. And drinking enough liquids is also a problem . . . even water is difficult. A mixture of water and Gatorade seems to work the best. He is very weak, and I have to assist him in much of what we took for granted just a few months ago.
>
> I have had to buy him all new clothes twice. . . . The hospice people came yesterday for an initial visit. . . . Right now things are very difficult. I feel as though the hosts of hell have been unleashed against us to bring worry, frustration, confusion, and to attempt to make us doubt all we believe. But, in the words of an old song, "Christ has regarded our helpless estate, and has shed his own blood for our souls!" And in Him we live and

move and have our being, and are able to withstand the onslaught of the enemy. Underneath the anguish is the deep peace of God that passes all understanding.[7]

God's peace isn't the absence of conflict or the nonexistence of problems. It is the Gulf Stream of His grace below the surface levels of life. We lay hold of the transcendent peace of the God of peace, which can stabilize our thoughts and emotions in every situation. That's God's ironclad promise to those who put Philippians 4:4–6 into practice. Verse 7 says, "And the peace of God, which transcends all understanding, will guard your hearts and your minds in Christ Jesus."

THE GOD OF PEACE

But the Lord doesn't stop with that. The passage develops, progresses, and rises higher as we continue through it. Verse 8, as we've seen, continues, "Finally, brothers and sisters, whatever is true . . . noble . . . right . . . pure . . . lovely . . . admirable . . . excellent or praiseworthy—think about such things." And verse 9 brings another promise to us—one that's even greater than the promise of God's peace: "Whatever you have learned or received or heard from me, or seen in me—put it into practice. *And the God of peace will be with you.*"

The only thing better than the *peace of God* is the *God of peace*, who promises to be with us forever. This harkens back to verse 5: "The Lord is near . . . the God of peace will be with you." Imagine! Having the peace of God within you, and the God of peace beside you.

Perhaps you've noticed during our excursion through Philippians 4:4–9 that it's like hiking over two summits. The pathway of Philippians 4:4–7 leads higher and higher until we arrive at the overlook of the peace of God. Then we begin again with verse 8 and ascend to an even greater summit in verse 9 with the God of peace. We can chart it like this:

SUMMIT 1
Verses 4–7

- Rejoice always;
- Be gentle;
- Recall the Lord's nearness;
- Do not be anxious;
- Pray in every situation . . .
- *with thanksgiving*;
The peace of God
will guard your
hearts and minds
in Christ Jesus.

SUMMIT 2
Verses 8–9

- Think on whatever is
true, noble, right, pure,
lovely, admirable,
excellent, and praiseworthy;
- And put into practice
what you learn from others;
The God of peace
will be
with you.

Throughout the Bible, we see God portrayed as the ever-present God of peace. There's an interesting story in the book of Judges, for example. When the Lord appeared to Gideon to commission him for His work, Gideon was alarmed. He realized he had seen the angel of God, which was tantamount to seeing God Himself, and he was agitated. He expected to die. But the Lord spoke to him aloud, saying, "Peace! Do not be afraid. You are not going to die" (Judges 6:23). Judges 6:24 says, "So Gideon built an altar to the LORD there and called it The LORD Is Peace."

A more literal translation of this is "Jehovah-Shalom," or "Yahweh-Shalom," and it's one of the great biblical names for God: The Lord Is Peace. That is one of His many great titles in Scripture.

The priestly benediction in Numbers 6 says, "The LORD turn his face toward you and give you peace" (v. 26). Similarly is the benediction at the end of 2 Thessalonians: "Now may the Lord of peace himself give you peace at all times and in every way. The Lord be with all of you" (3:16).

Likewise, 1 Thessalonians 5:23 says, "May God himself, the God of peace, sanctify you through and through." If the God of peace is sanctifying us through and through, growing us, developing us, and making us more spiritual and more holy, it only makes sense that we would experience more of His peace throughout the process.

I've quoted a lot of verses in this chapter, and when we pull them all together we have a stockpile of Scripture reinforcing the twin truths of Philippians 4 about the peace of God and the God of peace. Let's review them once more, and you might circle the one that speaks most to you as you read them. Doing so will help you begin the practice of peace today:

- "Thou wilt keep him in perfect peace, whose mind is stayed on thee: because he trusteth in Thee. Trust ye in the LORD forever; for in the LORD JEHOVAH is everlasting strength."
- He called the altar Jehovah-Shalom—the Lord is peace.
- "Peace I leave with you; My peace I give you. I do not give you as the world gives. Do not let your hearts be troubled and do not be afraid."
- "Therefore, since we have been justified through faith, we have peace with God through our Lord Jesus Christ."
- "He was pierced for our transgressions, He was crushed for our iniquities; the punishment that brought us peace was on Him."
- "He Himself is our peace."
- "I have told you these things, so that in Me you may have peace. In this world you will have trouble. But take heart! I have overcome the world."
- "Great peace have those who love Your law, and nothing can make them stumble."
- "May God himself, the God of peace, sanctify you through and through."
- "Now may the Lord of peace himself give you peace at all times and in every way."

Grow familiar with these verses and remind yourself of them if you feel guilty whenever a ray of peace shines through your heart and dispels a cloud of anxiety. Sometimes I think to myself, *If I have peace of mind, I must be out of my mind. I have a responsibility to worry; and how can I, in good conscience, go around without, as Havergal put it, a surge of worry, a shade of care, or a blast of hurry? I need the adrenaline of anxiety to solve this crisis.*

Biblical peace isn't a lighthearted, devil-may-care attitude of frivolity. It takes life seriously, and it's aware of the gravity of any situation. But when peace rules in the heart, the soul is anchored in the storms. It isn't the adrenaline of anxiety we need, but the Prince of Peace. Peace and strength are siblings; they are twins. Psalm 29:11 says, "The LORD gives strength to his people; the LORD blesses his people with peace."

Notice the words "his people." Our peace depends on a relationship with God through Jesus Christ. The most important phrase in Philippians 4:4–9 is made up of the three words we find at the end of verse 7: "in Christ Jesus." This was Paul's signature line. In reading through his letters in the New Testament, we see this phrase again and again—in Christ, in Christ, in Christ! All our blessings are in Him. All our hope is in Him. All our peace is in Him, and He is our very life. "And the peace of God, which transcends all understanding, will guard your hearts and your minds in Christ Jesus."

I recently had the opportunity to speak at a Christian gathering in Interlaken, Switzerland. After the second or third night, I noticed an elderly woman on the second row listening intently throughout my message. The next night I went up and spoke to her. Shortly afterward someone asked me, "Do you know who that was—the woman to whom you were speaking?"

"No, I don't."

My friend said, "That woman is the last surviving member of Winston Churchill's secret corps of spies."

During World War II, Churchill bypassed the British intelligence service, MI6, and he secretly recruited an army of spies who operated directly under his authority. They were primarily saboteurs. Few people in the government knew of their existence, though, at its zenith, there were about thirteen thousand people involved. This nest of spies was headquartered in a building on Baker Street, and they sometimes were called the Baker Street Irregulars.

This woman—Noreen Riols—was the last of them.

The next night after the service I asked if I could talk with her. She was very friendly and willing to talk. She told me that for sixty years following the war, she had not been allowed to tell anyone what she had done. The British government kept the existence of Churchill's Secret Army a classified secret until the year 2000. Even her own mother didn't know the truth of it, but had always thought Noreen had worked for the Ministry of Agriculture and Fish during the war.

When the official records were unsealed in 2000, Noreen could finally talk about her experiences. She was only a teenager when recruited, and she worked on British soil, training and helping support the saboteurs. She fell in love with one of the secret agents. "He was a very brave man," she said. "He was going on a last dangerous mission and they said, 'Only he can do it. If anyone can pull it off, he can.' But he was too well-known. He should never have gone. He promised me that this was his last mission, really his last. But he didn't come back."

All she had of him was a picture, which she kept in the back of her billfold until it was stolen; then she had nothing of him.

When the war ended, she said, it was difficult trying to return to normal. She was now unemployed and unable to tell anyone what she had done. It was a rough transition, and as time went by she tumbled into depression. At the age of forty, she had an abortion, which, she said, did her in. "I fell into a terrible, terrible depression. I was twice in a psychiatric hospital and was about to go in for the third time. But I said, 'No, no, I'm not going back.' Some dear friends came and said, 'Look, these medications are not helping, and you are taking more and more of them.'"

Noreen's friends started praying earnestly for her, and she agreed to let them pray for her. But there followed what she called "terrible months of miseries and grayness and blackness . . . I came to the end of myself; and when you come to the end of yourself there really isn't anywhere else to go, is there? I was suicidal, by the way. It was awful."

But then, through the witness of her friends, she came to the knowledge of the Lord and found Jesus Christ as her Savior. That's when everything changed. "He gave me peace, which is something I hadn't had for a long time," she said, "and then gradually life became beautiful again."[8] For many years, she has faithfully attended Bible conferences and grown in her love for Scripture and the peace it brings her through Christ. That's why she had come to Interlaken, and that's how I met her.

Jesus summed up all this in John 16:33: "I have told you these things, so that in me you may have peace. In this world you will have trouble. But take heart! I have overcome the world." And—one more verse—Psalm 119:165 says, "Great peace have those who love your law, and nothing can make them stumble."

This is the normal Christian experience—guarded around the clock by the peace of God and walking every moment with the God of peace.

I don't want to dissuade you from seeking medical help or quality counseling as you deal with the difficult issues of life. As I said in the preface, many gifted people can help us with our struggles in life, and I thank God for skilled professionals who come alongside us with their support, therapy, medical skill, and psychological resources. Yet we know the best help in the world will be tremendously enhanced by the truths of Philippians 4, but will be diminished without the dogged practice of the habits found in these ancient verses.

You've been worried long enough. Let the Lord Jesus Christ have complete control over your life and over all your problems and concerns, every one of them. Rejoice in Him. Be gentle. Practice His nearness. Don't worry about anything but pray about everything. Find items for which to be thankful. Meditate on God's Word. Learn from others and follow the example of those who trust Him fully.

Gradually life will become beautiful again, the peace of God will guard your thoughts and emotions—a peace that transcends all understanding. Marvelous peace. Perfect peace. Multiplied peace. For the Lord gives strength to His people; He blesses His people with peace.

DISCUSSION QUESTIONS

1. Read Psalm 23. Which of these verses describe scenes of peace? What about the green pastures and still waters of verse 2? What about the

darkest valley in verse 4? Is there as much transcendent peace in verse 4 as in verse 2? What does this tell us about the peace of God?

2. According to Psalm 29:10–11, what benefits come to us from God's heavenly throne? What's the relationship between these benefits and great gifts? How does one lead to the other?

3. Notice again the three little words at the end of Philippians 4:7: "And the peace of God, which transcends all understanding, will guard your hearts and your minds *in Christ Jesus.*" Make sure you've given your life to Him, confessing your sins, receiving Him as Savior, and acknowledging Him as Lord. This is the beginning of the life that buries worry in the vacated tomb of Jesus. If you aren't sure of your relationship with God, offer this simple prayer and follow it up with the truths you've learned in this chapter:

Dear God, I know You love me and I believe Christ died to give me peace with You and inner peace in my heart. I confess my sins. With Your help, I will turn from them. I here and now receive Jesus Christ as my Savior and Lord. I thank You for this moment, in Jesus' name. Amen.

CONCLUSION

"DON'T WORRY ABOUT IT!"

When I spent a few days with my friends Reese and Linda Kauffman at their home in Telluride, Colorado, I was working on a project. One afternoon Reese suggested we explore some of the old mining trails in the Rockies in his off-road vehicles. Just as we got ready to leave, a terrific thunderstorm blew in and I saw a bolt of lightning strike a tree across the valley. It sent up a plume of smoke. Linda and I looked at each other, and I said, "Reese, are you sure we should go out in this weather?"

He said, "Don't worry about it." So off we went in his truck to a remote trailhead where we unloaded his open-air, all-terrain vehicle and started up old mining roads, along narrow switchbacks, alongside deep drop-offs, higher and higher, until we crossed a high mountain pass at about fourteen thousand feet. Along the way the weather grew worse, and when we reached the highest elevations we found ourselves in the middle of an electrical storm.

Reese pulled out a couple of ponchos and handed one to me. Reese is fearless but I'm not. So I said, "Reese, are we safe in this contraption?" He may not have liked my calling his vehicle a contraption, but he shrugged it off, glanced around at the storm, and said, "Don't worry about it."

But I did worry about it with a growing foreboding. Lightning and thunder surrounded us, and we were pelted by rain and hail. The sky was rumbling like a bowling alley. I said, "Reese, I know that if a person is in a car during a thunderstorm, the tires serve as insulation. At least that's what I've been told. But I've always been under a roof. What about a vehicle like this with no top or anything? Do you think we're safe?"

He shrugged and said, "Don't worry about it." I think he might have also mentioned something about the Lord protecting us, but he was drowned out by a thunderclap, and I didn't hear much of that part. I looked around for an overhanging rock or a crevice, but there was no rock of ages cleft for me. So I told Reese I didn't think we were very safe in the storm. What if lightning struck us? We were in a remote pace where no one would find us. The air was thin, the weather was turning, and the storm was closing in.

Reese turned to me, and his blue eyes turned to a rather cold shade that I'd never seen before, and he said slowly and deliberately, like a parent instructing a child: "Don't worry about it!"

I decided to try not worrying about it. I put on my poncho, gripped the edge of my seat, and surrendered myself to whatever happened. The storm passed, of course, and swept away some of the clouds. The sun peeked out and the views were fabulous. By then, it was rather late and I had another battle with fear as Reese barreled down the mountain at breakneck speed, traveling the last half of the trip in darkness along treacherous crags and rocks, with the temperature plunging by the minute. By then I was too tired and cold to . . . well, to worry about it.

Later I told that story at an event where Reese was present, and a few weeks later I received a package in the mail. It was a very nice polo shirt from Reese, embossed with the words: "Don't worry about it."

I don't want to compare Reese Kauffman with the voice at Sinai, but quite often since then, when caught in the various storms of life, I hear those words echoing in my ear: "Don't worry about it." After all, that's very nearly what the Lord is telling us in Philippians 4, and it takes real emotional discipline to respond in faith: "Don't worry about anything; instead, pray about everything" (Philippians 4:6 NLT).

It's not a flippant message. The dangers are real enough, the storms are fierce, and, humanly speaking, there's cause for alarm. But God isn't speaking humanly. He is divinely speaking, and His words are backed by His authority. Imagine God speaking those words audibly to you the next time your stomach churns, your muscles tense, your breathing quickens, and you feel a wave of worry wash over you. The Lord really speaks to us in a still, small voice, whispering: "Don't worry about it. Don't worry about anything."

Remember, the key isn't totally avoiding the outbreak of anxiety. Even having committed Philippians 4:4–9 to memory and having meditated on it over and over, I can't be certain I'll never again fall into the ditch of anxiety. I'm quite sure I will, and probably very soon. To me, worry comes as naturally as breathing. But I am committed to using this passage as a basis for victory.

With time and maturity, we'll learn to deal more quickly with sudden onsets of anxiety, and the real secret to burying worry is learning to instinctively mobilize the truths of Philippians 4:4–9 when those anxious moments do arise. Think of these verses as a squadron of combat-ready fighter jets, ready to scramble at the least provocation. That's how we must learn to use them.

The apostle Paul takes pains to describe this as a learning process. Just a few verses later, in Philippians 4:11–13, he added: "I have learned to be content whatever the circumstances. . . . I have learned the secret of being content in any and every situation. . . . I can do all this through him who gives me strength."

The word *content* is akin to the word *peace* used earlier in the chapter, and this is something we must learn, for it doesn't come naturally. We have to "practice these things." It's a learned way of life, one that Paul learned himself before passing along the lessons to us in Philippians 4.

He ended the passage by saying, "And my God will meet all your needs according to the riches of his glory in Christ Jesus. To our God and Father be glory forever and ever. Amen" (Philippians 4:19–20).

And that's our great goal—not simply to worry less and live more, but to do so in order to bring glory to the God who has promised to meet all our needs out of the riches of His glory.

If you've read any of my other books, you know I appreciate the great songs of the Christian faith. My Then Sings My Soul series tells the remarkable stories behind many of these treasured hymns. I'd like to end this chapter by sharing a hymn story that isn't in my other volumes. It has to do with Pastor Warren Cornell, a Methodist Episcopal clergyman who labored from Wisconsin to Texas in the nineteenth century.

In 1889, Cornell was involved in evangelistic meetings near West Bend, Indiana, and one day he seemed especially pensive and introspective. Perhaps he was battling anxiety or discouragement. Sitting in the tent where the meetings were held, he jotted some words on the back of an advertising folder. But as he left the tent, he dropped the paper. An hour or two later, musician William G. Cooper entered the tent, saw the paper, and picked it up. Reading the words, Cooper realized Cornell had been trying to compose a poem about the peace of God. Cooper was touched by the fragmented lines. He filled in some of the words and thoughts until he had a complete poem, then he set it to music.

Shortly afterward, Cornell and Cooper published their hymn, "Wonderful Peace," reportedly for five dollars. It became one of the most comforting gospel songs of the twentieth century—a century ravaged by a great depression, two world wars, and a struggle for civil rights. It was especially beloved in African American churches, and somehow it brought people together. It was often sung at church when I was growing up, and I remember hearing my mother sing it when I was a child. Since it has a cherished place in my heart, I wanted to leave it with you as a prayer for us as we implement the truths of Philippians 4.

May God bless you with His wonderful peace that passes all understanding.

> Far away in the depths of my spirit tonight
> Rolls a melody sweeter than psalm;
> In celestial-like strains it unceasingly falls
> O'er my soul like an infinite calm.

CONCLUSION

Peace, peace, wonderful peace,
Coming down from the Father above!
Sweep over my spirit forever, I pray
In fathomless billows of love.[1]

A CLOSING THOUGHT

An Alternative Reading to Philippians 4:4–9
from the Devil's Everyday Version (DEV)

Doubt in the Lord always. I will say it again: Doubt! Let your fretfulness be evident to all. The Lord has forgotten you. Be anxious about everything, and in every situation, by mistrust and misery, with thanklessness, wring your hands before God. And the weight of the world, which transcends all understanding, will grip your hearts and minds as you lose your grip on Christ Jesus.

Finally, brothers and sisters, whatever is aggravating, whatever is agitating, whatever is alarming, whatever is threatening, whatever is upsetting, whatever is unnerving—if anything is disquieting and disturbing—think about such things.

Whatever you have learned or received or heard from me, or seen in me—ignore. And the God of peace will elude you.[1]

ANOTHER CLOSING THOUGHT

How to Bury Worry

Philippians 4:4–9

Rejoice in every circumstance,
Be gentle; God is near.
In every daily happenstance,
Refuse to live in fear.
But pray instead. With trusting heart
try gratitude and praise,
for God has promised to impart
His peace through all your days.
So think of Him amid the hurry;
follow heroes who are true,
then you can learn to bury worry—
before worry buries you.

—Robert J. Morgan

ACKNOWLEDGMENTS

I didn't work back through this manuscript to count the number of Bible verses used in this book, but they are the only infallible words on these pages. I want to begin by acknowledging with deepest gratitude what a privilege God has given us to be lifelong students of His Word!

The Lord also blessed me with a wife who doesn't worry as much as I do. Katrina's robust faith in the Lord has anchored our marriage and helped me through the rougher patches of life. She and I are also blessed with three dearest daughters—Victoria, Hannah, and Grace—and their wonderful families. I love them for putting up with me and my deadlines.

I'm also pleased to be working with Matt Baugher of HarperCollins Christian Publishing, and with Daisy Hutton and her incredible team at W Publishing Group, including my senior editor, Paula Major. They're the best in the business, and, as I know from experience, their greatest aim is to advance the message of the gospel.

Sealy and Matt Yates have been a father–son tag team as my literary agents, and I'm thankful to Yates & Yates for representing me with keen insight and relentless service. And to Sherry Anderson, Casey Pontious, and the congregation of the Donelson Fellowship in Nashville, where these chapters were born as sermons.

And to faithful readers like you, without whom writers like me would be useless.

Thank you!

STUDY GUIDE FOR INDIVIDUAL AND GROUP USE

TEN LESSONS

This study uses the New International Version
but can be adapted for other translations.

WELCOME TO OUR STUDY!

If you've read Robert J. Morgan's books, you know they're packed with Scripture. He believes the lines of Scripture are where the electricity flows between heaven and earth, and between God and us. Psalm 119:130 says, "The unfolding of your words gives light."

This study guide is designed to take you deeper into the Bible's wonderful passages about combating worry and cultivating peace of mind and heart. All you need is an open Bible and a pencil. Please visit robertjmorgan.com/worry-less for a free downloadable copy of this study guide.

After reading a chapter in Dr. Morgan's book *Worry Less, Live More*, go deeper into its contents—either in personal or group study—by working through the following questions, answers, scriptures, and insights. Each lesson divides into three sections: *Start Up*, which introduces the subject; *Drill Down*, which takes you deeper into the Scripture; and *Carry On*, which provides some practical takeaways. The nine lessons in this book correspond to the eight chapters in *Worry Less, Live More*, plus an introductory lesson based on the preface and introduction of the book. You can add a tenth lesson by devoting a final session to testimonies and fellowship, and by preparing a devotional or lesson on the last half of Philippians 4, focusing on Philippians 4:10–20.

For more resources, visit www.robertjmorgan.com.

May the Lord bless you in this study. Let's begin with a prayer:

Dear Father, if You had Your complete and perfect way within me,
I wouldn't worry about anything, but I would trust Your absolute

*control over everything, large and small, in my life. But, Lord, I'm not
there yet. So I ask You to open Your Word to me and open my mind
to Your Word. May each verse, each question, and each insight be a
stepping-stone in helping me to worry less and live more. May Your
great antianxiety passage of Philippians 4:4–9 become exemplified in
me as never before, and then may I share the secrets with others. I pray
with thanksgiving and in the name of Christ Jesus. Amen.*

INTRODUCTORY LESSON

Based on the preface and introduction of *Worry Less, Live More*

Start Up

How much do you worry? On a scale from one to ten, with ten being
the highest, what's your anxiety quotient?

Do you worry constantly or occasionally?

Do you battle panic attacks or PTSD?

What is worrying you most right now?

Does someone close to you struggle with anxiety issues? How is it
affecting him or her? How is it affecting you?

Drill Down

Read 2 Corinthians 2:2–11 and 7:5–7. Do you agree the apostle Paul was high-strung and subject to anxiety?

If Paul, who was a student of the Old Testament, had come to you looking for answers to help him cope with his worries, do you have any passages you would have suggested? Imagine you were counseling Paul. Where might you have urged him to turn in the Old Testament for reassurance and strength? Check out these possibilities:

- Joshua 1:7–9
- Psalm 4
- Isaiah 40:27–31

Read Philippians 4:4–9 below. Taking a pencil or pen, draw a slash after every period, and notice how the passage divides into nine sentences. Now circle the two occurrences of the word *peace*. Using your pencil or pen, make other notes, circles, underlines, boxes, marks, or shades, indicating interesting observations that come to you as you read this passage over and over. Note and underscore the verbs, which represent the commandments or injunctions given.

Rejoice in the Lord always. I will say it again: Rejoice! Let your gentleness be evident to all. The Lord is near. Do not be anxious about anything, but in every situation, by prayer and petition, with thanksgiving, present your requests to God. And the peace of God, which transcends all understanding, will guard your hearts and your minds in Christ Jesus. Finally, brothers and sisters, whatever is true, whatever is noble, whatever is right, whatever is pure, whatever is lovely, whatever is admirable—if anything is excellent or praiseworthy—think about such things. Whatever you have learned or received or heard from me, or seen in me—put it into practice. And the God of peace will be with you.

What new insights presented themselves as you analyzed this passage?

Now look up 2 Thessalonians 3:16. How is this verse similar to and different from Philippians 4:4–9?

Carry On

This lesson surveyed a number of encouraging passages in Scripture. Choose one phrase from one of the verses you looked at, and write that phrase here:

Why does this phrase speak to you so deeply?

Make it a point to repeat that phrase often. You might try saying it five times before bed, five times when arising, and five times at some point during the day. Set reminders on your phone if necessary. Write it on a card if you need to. Let that phrase permeate your thinking for the coming week, and share it with those with whom you come in contact. Let it become your biblical slogan for the coming week.

CHAPTER ONE: THE PRACTICE OF REJOICING

Start Up

If you have access to online recordings, play a sample of the song "Don't Worry Be Happy" by Bobby McFerrin. Now find and play a verse of the great hymn "Rejoice, the Lord Is King" by Charles Wesley. In terms of musical style, these are obviously different kinds of songs, but the biggest difference isn't in the music or rhythm but in the message. Discuss the contrast in philosophy between the two songs. Which do you think provides a stronger basis for a joyful life? Why?

Drill Down

Read Philippians 3:1 and 4:4.

Now turn to Acts 16 and study the founding of the Philippian church in verses 11–40. Do you see how the joy that pervades the letter of Philippians was on display during the founding of the church, even amid pain and persecution? Where in Acts 16 is the expression of joy the greatest?

Look up the expression "rejoice in the LORD" in Habakkuk 3:17–19. What does this tell us about our capacity of rejoicing when everything seems to be going wrong?

- Have you ever had a Habakkuk 3 period in your life, in which you were able to rejoice even when things appeared to be falling apart?

Why are the words "in the Lord" so important to the phrase "rejoice in the LORD"? Dr. Morgan lists some of the qualities about God in which we can rejoice, linking them all together with the letter *P*. Go ahead and list them:

- His Presence
- His P_____ & _____
- His P_____
- His P_____
- His P_____ & _____
- His Provision
- His P_____
- His P_____

Circle the item in the list above that means the most to you right now. Can you think of other qualities, attributes, or blessings connected with God that could be added to this list?

Carry On

In chapter 1 of *Worry Less, Live More*, Dr. Morgan says that rejoicing in the Lord is: (1) a command we obey, (2) a choice we make, (3) a condition we cultivate, and (4) a climate we create. As we do these things, we begin living life with an enthusiasm that uplifts others. Have your day-by-day attitudes lifted others up, or have you been dragging them down? Is there a practical idea from this chapter you can implement this week?

In what little area can you be more enthusiastic this week?

If you were to choose to rejoice, what would that look like or feel like right now in your life? How can you start doing that now? Finish this study by reading James 1:2 and asking the Lord to cultivate in you a perpetual spirit of joy and rejoicing.

CHAPTER TWO: THE PRACTICE OF GENTLENESS

Start Up

Just for fun, imagine you were an ancient scribe who had a copy of Philippians 4:4–9, but some words were missing in verse 5. You had no idea Paul had written the words "let your gentleness be evident to all." That sentence had been damaged in your scroll, and you had to compose some words to fill in the blank. What would you have chosen for a logical connecting sentence at that point? Use your imagination and try to think like an ancient scholar who had to reconstruct a missing part of the passage. Insert your words below:

Rejoice in the Lord always. I will say it again: Rejoice! _____

_____ _____ _____ _____ _____

_____ _____ _____ _____. The Lord is near.
Do not be anxious about anything, but in every situation, by prayer
and petition, with thanksgiving, present your requests to God. And
the peace of God, which transcends all understanding, will guard your
hearts and your minds in Christ Jesus. Finally, brothers and sisters,
whatever is true, whatever is noble, whatever is right, whatever is pure,
whatever is lovely, whatever is admirable—if anything is excellent or
praiseworthy—think about such things. Whatever you have learned
or received or heard from me, or seen in me—put it into practice. And
the God of peace will be with you.

Perhaps you would have written a sentence explaining joy a bit more, or
perhaps you would have said something about faith. Imagine inserting
one of these phrases from Psalm 100: "Worship the Lord with gladness"
or "Know that the Lord is God" or "We are his people, the sheep of his
pasture" or "Enter his gates with thanksgiving."
Why did Paul instead insert a sentence about gentleness?

Now look at the text again and draw lines between the words *gentle* in
verse 5, *peace* in verse 7, *peace* in verse 9, and *lovely* in verse 8. These words
are not synonyms, but do you see how they convey a similar atmosphere?

Rejoice in the Lord always. I will say it again: Rejoice! Let your gentleness
be evident to all. The Lord is near. Do not be anxious about anything, but
in every situation, by prayer and petition, with thanksgiving, present your
requests to God. And the peace of God, which transcends all understanding, will guard your hearts and your minds in Christ Jesus. Finally,
brothers and sisters, whatever is true, whatever is noble, whatever is
right, whatever is pure, whatever is lovely, whatever is admirable—if anything is excellent or praiseworthy—think about such things. Whatever

you have learned or received or heard from me, or seen in me—put it
into practice. And the God of peace will be with you.

Drill Down

Let's trace the word *gentleness* through Scripture, looking at a number
of passages in which the word occurs. Look up the following verses and
write a brief statement describing what they say about being gentle:

- Proverbs 15:1 _____
- Proverbs 25:15 _____
- Matthew 11:29 _____
- Galatians 5:22–23 _____
- Ephesians 4:2 _____
- Colossians 3:12 _____
- 1 Timothy 3:3 _____
- 1 Timothy 6:11 _____
- Titus 3:2 _____
- 1 Peter 3:4 _____
- 1 Peter 3:15 _____

Carry On

In this chapter, Dr. Morgan suggests that gentleness: (1) reduces anxiety,
(2) reflects Christ, (3) gets things done, and (4) pleases the Lord. He
lists several examples, including the owner of a clothing store in his
hometown and the legendary basketball coach John Wooden. Can you
think of someone in your experience who displays the biblical quality of
gentleness? In what way has this person influenced or affected you?

Would you describe yourself as a gentle person? What relationships in
your life need a calmer and kinder touch? List them below, and turn
the list into a prayer list—not just for the people you've listed but for
your own attitude and approach toward them:

- _____
- _____
- _____
- _____

Take the little phrase from Philippians 4:5 with you into the week. Write it on a card. Quote it to yourself throughout the day. Pray it into your life. Post it wherever you're most likely to be upset. *Let your gentleness be evident to all.*

CHAPTER THREE: THE PRACTICE OF NEARNESS

Start Up

Think of a time when the presence of someone startled you. Perhaps you thought you were alone, but when you looked up or turned around someone was unexpectedly there. How did you feel?

How you do think you'd feel if the ever-present God suddenly became visible to you? See Luke 24:36–43. What if that happened right now? How would it change what you're doing? Would it alter any habits in your life?

If we know the Lord is always present, should it matter whether or not we can visually see Him? Shouldn't our lives constantly reflect an awareness of His presence? Why is it difficult to bear this in mind?

Drill Down

In chapter 3, Dr. Morgan suggests the phrase "The Lord is near" in Philippians 4:5 is subject to two interpretations: (1) His coming is near, and (2) His presence is near. Which do you think was most on Paul's mind as he wrote this sentence?

Let's begin with the truth about the Lord's coming.

- Read 1 Thessalonians 4:13–18. Verse 13 tells us not to be uninformed or to grieve as others do, and verse 18 tells us to use this passage to encourage one another. What most encourages you about the truth of the Lord's second coming?

- Read Romans 8:18 and 2 Corinthians 4:17. How should we evaluate our worries and burdens in view of the Lord's return? What current burden can you view differently if you do so against the backdrop of heaven and eternal life?

Now let's go on to the truth about the Lord's abiding presence. Read Psalm 139:1–12. What does this tell us about God? About us?

- Dr. Morgan lists several categories of verses that speak of God's omnipresence around us: (1) the *nearness* verses, (2) the *presence* verses, (3) the *with* verses, and (4) the *close* verses. Scan the list again in chapter 3, and find one verse that would currently reign as your favorite on this subject. What does this particular verse speak to you?

- Dr. Morgan lists several examples of revival, periods of time in which the presence of God seemed magnified in certain locations. Have you ever had an experience along these lines?

Carry On

While we want to pray and prepare for revival, we should not simply wait for special manifestations of God's presence, for we walk by faith and not by sight. One of the greatest secrets to enjoying the abiding presence of the Lord is by developing a meaningful prayer life. Take your pencil and draw a line between the word *near* in the following two verses.

James 4:8: "Come near to God and he will come near to you."

Deuteronomy 4:7: "What other nation is so great as to have their gods near them the way the LORD our God is near us whenever we pray to him?"

What small habit can you begin, tweak, strengthen, or resume this week that will help you better recognize the abiding presence of God?

CHAPTER FOUR: THE PRACTICE OF PRAYER

Start Up

If you had a cell phone linked to the throne of God in heaven giving you instant access to God Himself whenever you turned it on, how would you feel? If you could call and discuss with Him any problem in your life, what would it be? What would you say to Him?

What do you think He would say to you today?

What passage of Scripture do you think He'd suggest you read?

Drill Down

We do have a hotline to heaven, which is why the Bible says in Philippians 4:6: "Do not be anxious about anything, but in every situation, by prayer and petition, with thanksgiving, present your requests to God." How open is your line to heaven? What most hinders your prayer life?

Dr. Morgan wrote: "Somehow the apostle Paul squeezed, condensed, and compressed two great chapters of the Bible, Psalm 37 and Matthew 6, into one incredible verse—Philippians 4:6—and every phrase of this verse is a wonder of psychology and spirituality."

Let's look closer at these two chapters. How do Paul's words in this verse reflect what David said in Psalm 37:1–9?

How do Paul's words reflect what Jesus said in Matthew 6:5–33?

Why do we find it difficult to "take our burdens to the Lord and leave them there"?

Carry On

Dr. Morgan describes three patterns of prayer we should practice: (1) everyday prayer, (2) D-Day prayer, and (3) throughout-the-day prayer. Of the three, which do you most frequently practice?

Do you have a story of answered prayer to share with someone else?

This week, try an experiment. It sounds a bit legalistic, but it won't hurt to try it as an experiment. Use the stopwatch on your phone and determine to pray, alone and aloud, for a certain number of minutes a day—ten minutes, for example. Many of the people in Scripture prayed aloud, but many modern Christians have gotten away from private oral prayer. Try this for a certain number of days and see if it begins to feel more natural with every passing day. Talk to the Lord as though He were standing or sitting there with you—for He is!

CHAPTER FIVE: THE PRACTICE OF THANKSGIVING

Start Up

List some great spiritual truths that can be summarized in only two words:

- Rejoice always!
- Praise God!
- Let's pray!
- Be strong!

Sometimes the greatest concepts require the fewest words. Now think of the power of the two words that appear between commas in Philippians 4:6: "with thansksgiving."

Think of a time in your life in which everything went wrong, but in the middle of it all, you found something, large or small, for which to be thankful. When and where was that? How did gratitude make a difference in your mood, morale, or perseverance?

Drill Down

In this chapter, Dr. Morgan talks about (1) the theology of gratitude, (2) the psychology of gratitude, and (3) the methodology of gratitude. As he also points out, Colossians immediately follows Philippians. Just as the concept of joy runs through the book of Philippians, the concept of thanksgiving runs through Colossians. In some ways, the book of Colossians is an exposition of the words "with thanksgiving" that occur in Philippians 4:6.

In Colossians 1:3–6, why did Paul thank God?

In Colossians 1:10–12, the Lord gives us several ways in which we can please Him. Let's list them. Verse 10 says, "so that you may live a life worthy of the Lord and please him in every way."

• Bearing fruit in _____
• Growing _____
• Being _____
• And joyfully _____

Why are these elements of particular interest to God?

How are you doing in these four areas? Which do you need to strengthen?

In Colossians 2:6–7, we have three more ways in which we're to live for God. The verse says, "So then, just as you received Christ Jesus as Lord continue to live your lives in him."

• Rooted and _____
• Strengthened _____
• And overflowing _____

What does that last phrase mean? What do such people look like? How do they act? Can you see how this would minimize their tendencies to worry?

In Colossians 3:15, what happens if we let the peace of Christ rule in our hearts?

In Colossians 3:17, how are we to do everything that we do each day? Can you imagine how your attitude would be different if you embodied this verse?

In Colossians 4:2, how does the Lord tell us to pray?

Carry On

In talking about the methodology of gratitude, Dr. Morgan lists ten suggestions for cultivating the habit of thanksgiving. Which of these could become a realistic plan in your life? Focus on one or two for this week. How can you begin today or tomorrow to implement this?

Do you have another idea that wasn't on the list?

What small step can you take right now to cultivate a thankful spirit?

CHAPTER SIX: THE PRACTICE OF THINKING

Start Up

We're reading about combat veterans from war zones who, once home, were startled by, say, a balloon bursting at a birthday party, which understandably triggered a panic attack. What incites your anxiety? If you battle traumatic stress, what keys you off? If you suffer occasional anxiety, what thoughts switch it on?

Describe a time when you could trace a direct line between what your mind was thinking and what your emotions were feeling. Do you think it's possible to change your feelings by changing your thoughts?

Read again or discuss some of the quotes Dr. Morgan gave in the opening pages of this chapter from both the Bible and non-Christian sources. Do you have a personal example of Proverbs 4:23 (GNT): "Be careful how you think; your life is shaped by your thoughts"?

How healthy, by and large, are your thoughts?

Drill Down

Read these three parallel passages on biblical meditation, and on the chart on the next page, list the promises given in each verse:

- Joshua 1:8
- Psalm 1:2–3
- James 1:25

Command	Promise
Joshua 1:8	
Keep this Book of the Law	Then . . .
Always on your lips;	
meditate on it day and night,	
So that you may be careful	
to do everything written in it.	
Psalm 1:2–3	
. . . whose delight is in the	That person is like . . .
law of the Lord and who meditates	
on his law day and night.	
James 1:25	
But whoever looks intently into	They will be . . .
the perfect law that gives freedom,	
and continues in it—not forgetting	
what they have heard, but doing it . . .	

Compare these three passages very carefully. One occurs near the beginning of the Bible, one in the middle, and one near the end of Scripture. Yet they exhort us to do the same thing with Scripture, and they all repeat the same essential set of promises. Can you see the significance?

How does the meditation of Scripture lead to the life God promises?

These verses are by Joshua, the psalmist, and James. How do you think the apostle Paul would have stated this promise? Is that what he was doing in Philippians 4:8?

Notice how the process of sanctification is further described in Romans 12:2. How would you summarize and state this biblical teaching in an original statement of your own?

Carry On

In his book *Reclaiming the Lost Art of Biblical Meditation,* Dr. Morgan says we should have Bible verses circulating in our minds like water through a well or oil through a machine.[1] List two or three habits you can develop to better practice the biblical instructions about the meditation of Scripture.

Is there a passage or a verse you can begin to memorize? What are the first steps for you, should you decide to develop a daily habit of Scripture memory?

CHAPTER SEVEN:
THE PRACTICE OF DISCIPLESHIP

Start Up

Name one or two people who had the greatest influence on you as mentors. Why were they so important, and what did you learn most from them?

Drill Down

Review Philippians 4:9, Philippians 3:17, and 1 Corinthians 11:1. Are these statements you would be comfortable making?

Think about Paul's discipleship of Timothy.

- Read Acts 16:1–6.
- How old do you suppose Timothy was?

- What implications can you draw from the description of his parents?

- Consult 2 Timothy 1:4–5 and 2 Timothy 3:14–15.

- What can we learn about Timothy from 1 Timothy 5:23?

- Based on these verses, how would you describe Timothy?

- How important was it that Paul came into Timothy's life when he did?

- What word does he use to describe Timothy in 1 Timothy 1, verses 2 and 18? What is the implication of that?

Study 2 Timothy 2:1–2.
- Notice the opening in verse 1. Why would Paul issue this command?

- Chart the chain of transmission given in verse 2.

  You have heard me say
  Entrust to reliable people
  Who will be able to teach others also

- Compare this with John 17:20.

What does Jesus tell us to do in Matthew 28:19?

What role can you see yourself having in this process? How can you be part of the chain of discipleship that is still being forged after two thousand years?

Carry On

Do you have or need a mentor? In what area of life? Do you have someone in mind who can help you advance to the next stage in your Christian experience?

What books have affected you most—or what books are on your to-read list?

Think of someone—a child, grandchild, student, friend, or even a stranger—whom you could see yourself influencing, given the opportunity. Who is it? Are there any steps you can take to spur on the process? What are they?

CHAPTER EIGHT: THE PRACTICE OF PEACE

Start Up

Close your eyes and imagine the most peaceful scene you can paint in your mind. When you think of *peace*, what images come into your thoughts? If you were an artist painting a scene of peace, what would you put on the canvas?

Look up Psalm 23:2. Does that provide a picture of peace?

What about Psalm 23:4?

Do an online search, see if you can find a copy of Jack E. Dawson's painting *Peace in the Midst of the Storm*. If you can't find the picture, there's an old story that describes the same concept. There once was a king who offered a prize to the artist who would paint the best picture of peace. Many artists tried. The king looked at all the pictures, but there were only two he really liked and he had to choose between them. One picture was of a calm lake. The lake was a perfect mirror, for peaceful towering mountains were all around it. Overhead was a blue sky with fluffy white clouds. All who saw this picture thought that it was a perfect picture of peace. The other picture had mountains, too, but these were rugged and bare. Above was an angry sky from which rain fell and in which lightning played. Down the side of the mountain tumbled a foaming waterfall. This did not look peaceful at all. But when the king looked, he saw behind the waterfall a tiny bush growing in a crack in the rock. In the bush a mother bird had built her nest. There, in the midst of the rush of angry water, sat the mother bird on her nest in perfect peace. Which of the paintings won the prize?

What does that tell us about genuine, spiritual inner peace?

Drill Down

In Psalm 4:8, God's peace enables us to _____.

In Psalm 29:10–11, what benefits come to us by God's sovereign enthronement in the heavens?

_____

In Psalm 85:8, what does God say when we listen to Him?

_____

According to Psalm 85:10, Peace is married to a wonderful spouse, and they kiss each other all the time. Who is that?

_____

What gives us "great peace" in Psalm 119:165?

_____

Proverbs 14:30 lists another great benefit of inner peace. It _____

_____.

According to Isaiah 26:3–4, what keeps us in perfect peace?

_____

What did Christ do to provide us with this kind of peace? Isaiah 53:5 says:

_____

How did Jesus describe the kind of peace He provides for His children, according to John 14:27?

_____

And in John 16:33?

_____

How is our mind described when it's governed by the Holy Spirit (Romans 8:6)?

_____

What should rule in our hearts (Colossians 3:15)?

_____

If you were an automobile whose radiator was supposed to be filled with liquid peace, would you be full? Half-full? Quarter-full? Or empty?

_____

Now, go back to Philippians 4:4–9. What needs to happen in your life so you can get a personality-altering grip on the practice of peace?

_____

Carry On

In our step-by-step guide to peace of mind, we've looked at rejoicing, gentleness, nearness, prayer, thanksgiving, meditation, and discipleship. According to Philippians 4:4–9, if those practices are forming in our lives, we should have a growing sense of peace. Do you have a growing sense of peace?

In your own experience, which of the eight practices outlined in *Worry Less, Live More* needs the most work? What one step can you take right now to improve?

Notice again the three little words at the end of verse 7: "And the peace of God, which transcends all understanding, will guard your hearts and your minds *in Christ Jesus.*" Make sure you've given your life to Him, confessing your sins, receiving Him as Savior, and acknowledging Him as Lord. This is the beginning of the life that buries worry in the vacated tomb of Jesus. If you aren't sure of your relationship with God, offer this simple prayer and follow it up with the truths you've learned in this chapter:

Dear God, I know You love me and I believe Christ died to give me peace with You and inner peace in my heart. I confess my sins. With Your help, I will turn from them. I here and now receive Jesus Christ as my Savior and Lord. I thank You for this moment, in Jesus' name. Amen.

Therefore, since we have been justified through faith,
we have peace with God through our Lord Jesus Christ.
—Romans 5:1

Note: You can add a tenth lesson by devoting a final session to testimonies and fellowship and/or preparing a devotional message or lesson on the last half of Philippians 4, focusing on verses 10–20. Also, make sure you check out Robert J. Morgan's other books with available study guides:

The Red Sea Rules: 10 God-Given Strategies for Difficult Times
Crisis 101 (video study series based on *The Red Sea Rules*)
Mastering Life Before It's Too Late
The Lord Is My Shepherd
Simple: The Christian Life Doesn't Have to Be Complicated

For more information, visit robertjmorgan.com.

NOTES

Preface

1. Stephanie Samuel, "Bible's Most Popular Verse Is 'Be Anxious for Nothing,' Says Amazon," *The Christian Post,* November 9, 2014, www.christianpost.com /news/bibles-most-popular-verse-is-be-anxious-for-nothing-says-amazon -129346/.

Introduction

1. Amy Spencer, "Amanda Seyfriend: The Most Down-To-Earth member of the Glam New Guard," *Glamour,* www.glamour.com/magazine/2010/03/amanda -seyfried-the-most-down-to-earth-member-of-the-glam-new-guard.
2. I came across this quotation long ago but do not know its original source; one option is the mystery novelist Arthur Somers Roche.
3. T. M. Luhrmann, "The Anxious Americans," *New York Times,* www.nytimes .com/2015/07/19/opinion/sunday/the-anxious-americans.html.
4. Richard Harris, "Could Your Child's Picky Eating Be a Sign of Depression?," *All Things Considered,* NPR, www.npr.org/sections/health-shots/2015/08/03 /428016725/could-your-childs-picky-eating-be-a-sign-of-depression.
5. Carolyn Gregoire, "The Surprising Link Between Gut Bacteria and Anxiety," *Huffington Post,* www.huffingtonpost.com/2015/01/04/gut-bacteria-mental -healt_n_6391014.html.
6. Andrew S. Fox, et al, "Intergenerational Mediators of Early-Life Anxious Temperament, Proceedings of the National Academy of Sciences," 112, no. 29, 9118-22, http://pnas.org/content/112/29/9118full.
7. Susanna Schrobsdorff, "The Kids Are Not All Right," *Time,* November 7, 2016, 44–47.

8. George Müller, *The Autobiography of George Müller* (New Kensington, PA: Whitaker House, 1984), 155.

9. Gretchen Rubin, *Better Than Before: What I Learned About Making and Breaking Habits* (New York: Broadway Books, 2015), Kindle location 70.

10. Ibid., Kindle location 155.

11. Ibid., Kindle location 215.

Chapter 1: The Practice of Rejoicing

1. "Don't Worry Be Happy," *Wikipedia*, en.wikipedia.org/wiki/Don%27t_Worry, _Be_Happy.

2. Samuel Bradburn, *Select Letters: Chiefly on Personal Religion, by the Rev. John Wesley* (New York: T. Mason and G. Lane, 1838), 14.

3. Phyllis Thompson, *Count It All Joy* (Wheaton, IL: Harold Shaw Publishers, 1978), 13.

4. Ibid., 14.

5. Ibid., back cover.

6. Joy Ridderhof, *Are You Rejoicing?* (Los Angeles, CA: Global Recordings Network, 1984), entry for day 1.

7. Katie Hoffman, *A Life of Joy* (n.p.: Ano Klesis Publishing, 2006), 150–51.

8. Harry Bollback, *Our Incredible Journey* (Schroon Lake, NY: Word of Life Fellowship, 2011), 33.

9. Ibid., 181.

Chapter 2: The Practice of Gentleness

1. Monica Cantilero, "Married for 75 Years Without a Single Fight," Christian Today, August 11, 2015, www.christiantoday.com/article/married.for.75.years .without.a.single.fight.us.christian.couple.gets.medias.attention/61583.htm.

2. Jessica Bringe, "Area Couple Celebrates 75 Years of Marriage," *WEAU News*, www.weau.com/home/headlines/Area-couple-celebrates-75-years-of-marriage -320981951.html.

3. Fred Smith, Sr., *Breakfast with Fred* (Ventura, CA: Regal, 2007), 48–49.

4. Helen Steiner Rice, *Poems of Faith* (Carmel, NY: Guideposts, 1981), 33–34.

5. Donna Kincheloe, *I Never Walk the Halls Alone* (Nashville, TN: ACW Press, 2007), 72–74.

6. Ibid.

7. Phil Mason, *Napoleon's Hemorrhoids: And Other Small Events That Changed the World* (New York: Skyhorse Publishing, 2009), 31.

8. Based on a conversation with Rocky Forshey; used with permission.

9. John Wooden, *The Essential Wooden* (New York: McGraw-Hill, 2007), 8–9.

10. Ibid.

11. Ibid., 11.

12. Quoted by Harold C. Lyon in *Tenderness Is Strength: From Machismo to Manhood* (New York: Harper & Row, 1977), 7.

Chapter 3: The Practice of Nearness

1. Maxwell Cornelius, "Sometime We'll Understand," hymn published in 1891.

2. This story appeared in numerous newspapers in September 1981, including *Gaffney Ledger*, September 4, 1981; *Schenectady Gazette*, September 4, 1981; *Daytona Beach Morning Journal*, September 4, 1981; and in Steve Petrone, "Woman, 85, Proves She's Tough-As-Nails After Her 4 Days in Horror Swamp," *Weekly World News*, September 29, 1981.

3. Frank Bartleman, *Azusa Street: An Eyewitness Account* (Alachua, FL: Bridge-Logos, 1980), 78.

4. Wesley Duewel, *Revival Fire* (Grand Rapids: Zondervan, 1995), 101.

5. Ibid., 134.

6. Ibid., 141, 183–84.

7. A. W. Tozer, *The Knowledge of the Holy* (New York: Harper & Row Publishers, 1961), 83.

8. William M. Anderson, *The Faith That Satisfies* (New York: Loizeaux Brothers, 1948), 165.

Chapter 4: The Practice of Prayer

1. Murat Halstead, *The Illustrious Life of William McKinley: Our Martyred President* (n.p.: Murat Halstead, 1901), 422.

2. James Ford Rhodes, *The McKinley and Roosevelt Administrations, 1897–1909* (New York: The Macmillan Company, 1922), 107. Not all scholars accept the historical accuracy of this story.

3. I recall hearing Vance Havner use a similar phrase years ago.

4. See the *New International Greek Testament Commentary*, for example.

5. Adapted from numerous newspaper articles, including "Fliers' Prayers Answered," www.nzherald.co.nz/nz/news/article.cfm?c_id=1&objectid=10511547; and "Pilot of Doomed Aircraft Claims That His Passenger's Prayers Helped the Pair Land Safely," www.dailymail.co.uk/news/article-1020917/Pilot-doomed-aircraft-claims-passengers-prayers-helped-pair-land-safely.html; and other similar articles.

6. J. Oswald Sanders, *Effective Prayer* (London: OMF International, 1961), 13.

7. Personal conversation with Dr. Don Wyrtzen and based on notes for his class on Worship and Prayer, delivered at Liberty University on October 8, 2015.

8. This account is based on numerous media stories, including James P. Moore, "American Prayers, On D-Day and Today," *Washington Post*, June 6, 2004, B03. Also see *The American Legion Magazine*, vol. 116–17, p. 81. Mark Batterson also researched this story and shared it in his book *ID: The True You* (Maitland, FL: Xulon Press, 2004), 88–89.

9. The original copy of this speech is displayed at the Franklin D. Roosevelt Presidential Library and Museum in Hyde Park, New York.

10. Cameron V. Thompson, *Master Secrets of Prayer* (Madison, GA: Light for Living Publications, 1990), 65.

11. Charles A. Tindley, "Leave It There," hymn published in 1916.

12. Michele Robbins, *Lessons from My Parents: 100 Moments That Changed Our Lives* (Sanger, CA: Familius, 2013), 4–5.

13. Ibid.

14. "Miracle Well Supplies Water for Troops in Desert Storm," *Tuscaloosa News*, August 22, 1992, based on Krulak's recounting the story at a luncheon sponsored by the Public Service Fellowship in Washington, DC.

Chapter 5: The Practice of Thanksgiving

1. Daniel Haun, "2013: What Should We Be Worried About? Global Cooperation Is Failing and We Don't Know Why," *Edge*, https://www.edge.org/response-detail/23773.

2. Peter Schwartz, "2013: What Should We Be Worried About? A World of Cascading Crises," *Edge*, https://www.edge.org/response-detail/23881.

3. John Tooby, "2013: What Should We Be Worried About? Unfriendly Physics, Monsters from the Id, and Self-Organizing Collective Delusions," *Edge*, https://www.edge.org/response-detail/23867.

4. Ibid.

5. Ruth Bell Graham, *It's My Turn* (Old Tappan, NJ: Fleming H. Revell Company, 1982), 136–37.

6. Ibid.

7. Albert Mohler, "Thanksgiving as a Theological Act," November 23, 2016, AlbertMohler.com, http://www.albertmohler.com/2016/11/23/thanksgiving-theological-act-mean-give-thanks/.

8. Quoted by Sally Clarkson and Sarah Clarkson in *The Lifegiving Home* (Carol Stream, IL: Tyndale House, 2016), 213.

9. Robert A. Emmons, *Thanks! How Practicing Gratitude Can Make You Happier* (Boston: Houghton Mifflin Company, 2007), 11.

10. Ibid., 22.

11. Ibid., 3.

12. Ibid., 11.

13. Janice Kaplan, *The Gratitude Diaries: How a Year Looking on the Bright Side Can Transform Your Life* (New York: Dutton, 2015), Kindle location 183.

14. Ibid., Kindle location 148.

15. Ibid., Kindle location 188–89.

16. Martin Rinkart, "Now Thank We All Our God," 1636, translated into English by Catherine Winkworth.

17. Linda Derby, *Life's Sticky Wick*, privately published manuscript, 2010. Used by permission.

18. Ibid.

19. Carmel Hagan, "The Secret to an Efficient Team? Gratitude," *99U.com*, http://99u.com/articles/37261/the-secret-to-an-efficient-team-gratitude.

20. E. A. Johnston, *J. Sidlow Baxter: A Heart Awake* (Grand Rapids: Baker Publishing Group, 2005), 124–26.

21. Ibid.

22. Ibid.

23. Ibid.

Chapter 6: The Practice of Thinking

1. Lillian Eichler Watson, *Light from Many Lamps* (New York: Simon and Schuster, 1951), 169–74.

2. "Ralph Waldo Emerson Quotes," Brainy Quote, accessed June 28, 2017, www.brainyquote.com/quotes/quotes/r/ralphwaldo108797.html.

3. Arthur L. Young, "Attitude and Altitude," *New Outlook: Volume 8, Number 11*, November, 1955, 42.

4. James Allen, *As a Man Thinketh* (New York: Barnes & Noble Books, 2002), 3, 22, 25.

5. Ibid., 43.

6. The Theosophical Society in America, *The Theosophical Quarterly*, 25 (1927), 185. I also relate this story in my devotional book, *All to Jesus*.

7. Ibid.

8. Quoted in J. I. Packer, *Knowing God* (Downers Grove: InterVarsity Press, 1973), 13.

9. Some of this material is adapted from my book *Reclaiming the Lost Art of*

Biblical Meditation (Nashville: HarperCollins, 2016), where the reader can find these ideas expanded into a variety of practical applications.

10. Geoffrey T. Bull, *When Iron Gates Yield* (Chicago: Moody Press), passim.

11. These insights came from attending an Institute of Basic Youth Conflicts seminar in the 1970s.

12. As told to Dr. Gary Mathena, director of practica for the School of Music at Liberty University, by his father, Dr. Harold Mathena.

Chapter 7: The Practice of Discipleship

1. *The Obstinate Horse and Other Stories from the China Inland Mission* (Shoals, IN: Kingsley Press, 2012), chapter 1.

2. Ibid.

3. Mary K. Crawford, *The Shantung Revival* (The Revival Library, www.revival-library.org), and Dennis Balcombe, *China's Opening Door* (Lake Mary, FL: Charisma House, 2014), 27.

4. William Wilberforce, *The Correspondence of William Wilberforce, Volume 1* (London: John Murray, 1840), 131–33.

5. Ibid.

6. "The Wisdom of Love" by Ian Maclaren, in *The Advance*, March 8, 1906, 298–99. This story is likely a fictional work by Maclaren, but it may well have been a fictionalized account of the experience of the Scottish pastor John Watson, who was best known by his pen name—Ian Maclaren. In other words, the story of John Carmichael seems to have been a fictionalized autobiography.

7. You can watch and listen to these lectures at buckhatchlibrary.com—and you'll be glad you did!

8. Bill Bright, *Revival Fires* (Orlando, FL: New Life Publications, 1995), 83–84.

Chapter 8: The Practice of Peace

1. Thomas Watson, *A Body of Practical Divinity* (Philadelphia: James Kay), 224.

2. Charles Haddon Spurgeon, *The Metropolitan Tabernacle Pulpit: Sermons Preached and Revised By C. H. Spurgeon During the Year 1890: Volume 36* (London: Passmore & Alabaster, u.d.), 421 and 430.

3. Annie Johnson Flint, "He Giveth More Grace," copyright 1941, renewed 1969 by Lillenas Publishing Company.

4. Based on conversations with Karen Singer and adapted from Hubert Mitchell, *The Story of a Nail* (Santa Clara, CA: Westmar Printing, Inc., 1978).

5. Frances Ridley Havergal, "Like a River Glorious," 1876.

6. Ibid.

7. Joyce Burlingame, *Living with Death, Dying with Life* (Bloomington, IN: Westbow, 2015), 130–31.

8. Based on a personal interview.

Conclusion: "Don't Worry About It!"

1. Warren D. Cornell and William G. Cooper, "Wonderful Peace," hymn published in 1889.

A Closing Thought

1. There is, of course, no "Devil's Everyday Version" except the one we experience for ourselves whenever we live in doubt and disobedience.

Welcome to Our Study!

1. Robert J. Morgan, *Reclaiming the Lost Art of Biblical Meditation* (Nashville: HarperCollins, 2016), xi.

ABOUT THE AUTHOR

Rob Morgan is the teaching pastor of The Donelson Fellowship in Nashville, Tennessee, where he has served for more than thirty-five years. He is a bestselling and Gold Medallion–winning writer of thirty books with more than four million in print. Rob has appeared on national television and radio shows and is available to speak at conferences, schools, churches, and events. He and his wife, Katrina, have three daughters and fourteen grandchildren.